AF394975

Love is...

A Story in Verse

Roy Benson

Cover & Illustrations

Christine Banat

First published 2023

Published under licence by Brown Dog Books and
The Self-Publishing Partnership Ltd, 10b Greenway Farm, Bath Rd,
Wick, nr. Bath BS30 5RL, UK

www.selfpublishingpartnership.co.uk

ISBN printed book: 978-1-83952-747-0
ISBN e-book: 978-1-83952-748-7

Printed and bound in the UK

This book is printed on FSC® certified paper

Love is.....

Roy Benson

Love is you

because you're you

Dedicated to Nancy

My Love

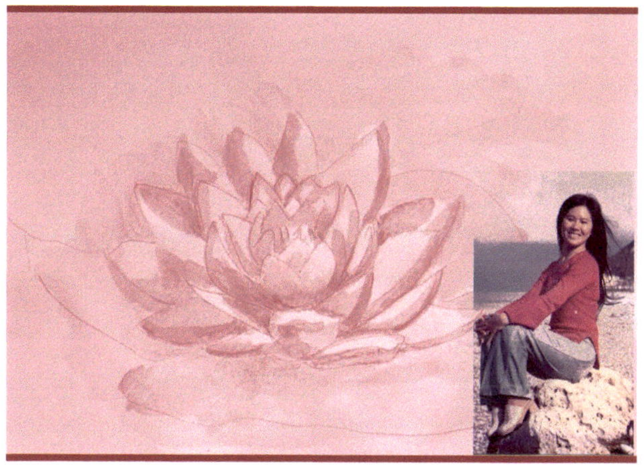

It is loving you that has given me the
movement to write these words of our
life and eternal love together

Paper fades with age

But words live on forever

LOVE

LOVE is KNOWING
LOVE is SHOWING
LOVE is ALWAYS GROWING
LOVE is SHARING
LOVE is CARING
LOVE is REUNITED
WITH A SMILE
LOVE is ALL THE WHILE

LOVE is HERE FOREVER
WITHOUT A SOUND
LOVE is HIGH ABOVE THE GROUND
LOVE is FLYING WITHOUT WINGS
LOVE is ALL IT BRINGS
LOVE is UNDISPUTED
LOVE is HOLDING ON
LOVE is NEVER GONE

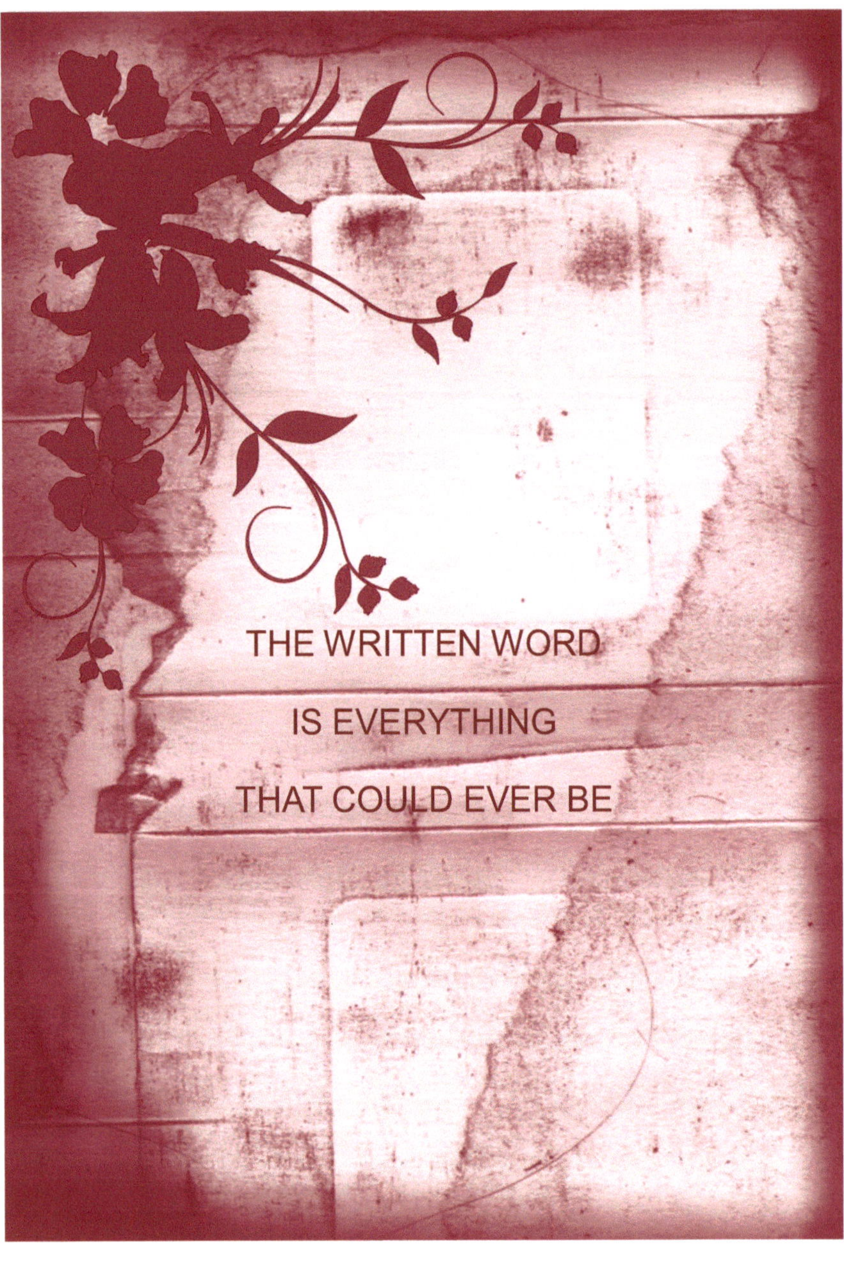

THE WRITTEN WORD
IS EVERYTHING
THAT COULD EVER BE

Index

Preface: LOVE

Love is	1
Slender as a Rose	5
Sometimes Love	8
The Girl With Eastern Eyes	10
NANCY NANCY LOVE NANCY	13
Trilogy in 4 Verses	16
Across The Oceans	18
MY SONG HAS NO MUSIC	23
LOVE YOU,YOU	27
YOU	28
You're All	30
There are Things	35
Turn to each other	38
If (one verse)	40
If I Could Find The Words	42
If Forever	44
One Day	46
My Love	47
TOGETHER	50
......More than......	53
Are We	58
...............For You	60
Beyond You	62
How	64
On a Bed of Roses	66
So in Love	68

Finding Love 71
Each Day by Day 73
Waiting 75
Many Love Songs 76
Many Love Days 78
Happiness 79
Being with You 84
Always 85
If (all the words) 89
Since Ancient Days 94
For Us 96
GOODBYE HELLO 100
If 101
Words 105
Times 106
I adore You 107
SUNSETS 109
I'll 114
MOUNTAINS 115
Touching 117
Sublime 118
This much love 119
Let's Turn a Page 123
I KNOW NOW 126
If Paradise 128
Do You Remember 130
LOVE 132
with LOVE 133
Remember 136
Love is Everything 137
BELIEVE IN 139
Just the 2 of us 146

Love is seashells in the sun
Love is loving everyone
Love is holding to the sky
A holy cross before your eye
Love is feeling warmest flesh
With the tenderness of hands
Love is loving all you can
Love is kissing every man
Love is being warm
On the coldest of days
Love is saying love
When its all you have to say
Love is kindness and affection
An arm across a shoulder
For someone very young
From someone who is older
Love is not a test
It's how you see life through
A living image of the way
Of all there is in you

Love is that special something
A feeling deep inside
The everything you cannot hide
Love is there it doesn't grow
Love is always loving
For all your love to show
Love cannot be found by searching
Or looking to the sky
Love is what is there
When a tear falls from your eye
Love is feeling for a moment
When a moment is one that's sad
Love is happy smiles
And always being glad
Love is knowing always growing
Through the many years
There are days when your loving
Is hiding certain fears
It's a new beginning every time
Love is you're always mine

Love is warmth and tenderness
Nothing more nothing less
Love is hotter than a fire
Burning with desire
Love is the closest touch
More than ever is
Or could be as much
All that glows from the moon
The words of every love song tune
The music that hits your heart
With every sunrise start
Love is you so much dearer
The wanting to be nearer
That sets the tingling shivers
Running up and down your spine
Love is you're always mine
Love is forever great
Part of life's eternal fate
Love is the start of spring
White lace and wedding ring

Love isn't in a book
Not there to be each look
Love is all that happens
From nowhere in a place
Love is finding someone
With that special face
Love is twenty clowns
In a circus ring
Love is all the happiness
with the laughter that they bring
Love is all the sense of being
In everything you've seen
It's not a shadow on the wind
Love is what has been
Love is always always
An end that never ends
Love is knowing when
Love is very precious
The most perfect gift to have

Love is all you're asked to give
Is that asking much at all

Slender as a Rose

Slender as a rose
You came along
And turned the time
Opened up the light
Sealed within my mind
And placed me forever
Upon cloud nine

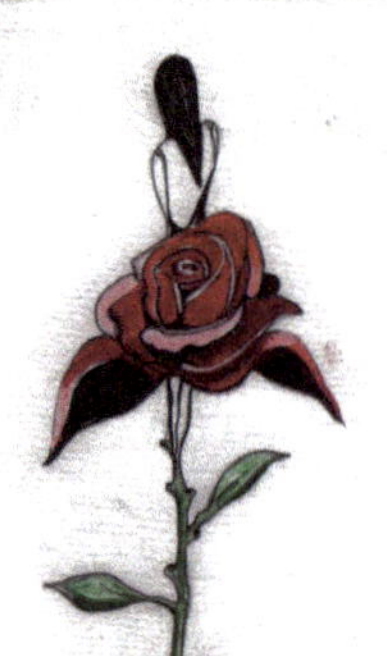

'I love her with all my heart

and shall look after her

with loving care always'

My Rose

You are my rose
The woman I chose
To give me a life
Of heavenly love

You are my rose
The woman I chose
To take me on a trail
Through a magic door

You held me close
Like no other can
We shared the freedom
Across enchanted land

You are my love
From the chosen few
You spoke with emotion
When you said I do

You are my rose

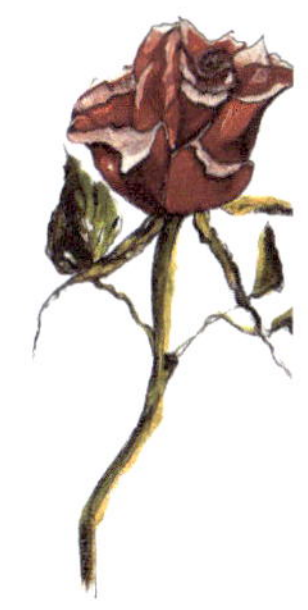

It was really lovely meeting you, going to the Classic Baker Street to see 'Taking Tiger Mountain By Storm'.

I cannot remember much about the movie as we were talking all the way through.

When we came out and I put my arm around your waist, holding your hand, a moment of magic went through me that I had never encountered before.

I knew something special had hit us, just as when Maria saw Tony across the dance floor for the first time in 'West Side Story'.

I do hope we can see each other again.

You are a very special person.

Sometimes Love

sometimes love you know
sometimes love you don't
sometimes love you can
sometimes love you won't

sometimes love was here
sometimes love was gone
sometimes love was off
sometimes love was on

sometimes love was instant
sometimes love was young
sometimes loves was old
I think my love has just begun

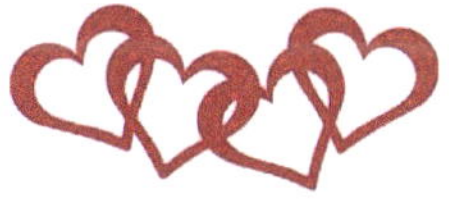

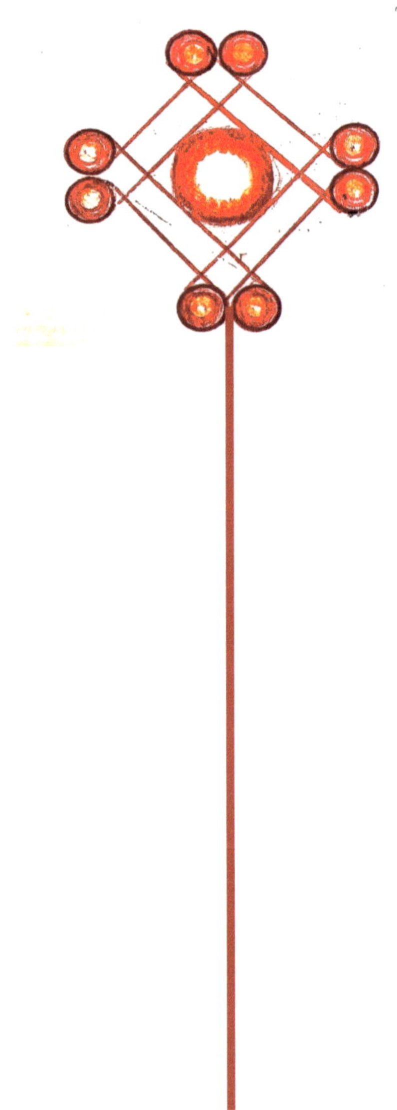

9

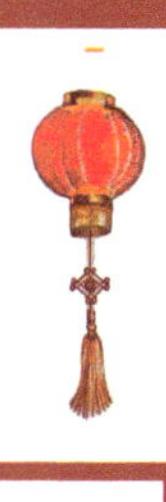

The Girl With Eastern eyes

As though from out a dream
The girl with eastern eyes
Brought me all my hellos
Sold me no goodbyes

A very special person
Warm with her today's
Making every moment
In all her special ways

Changing rain to sunshine
Within each clouded sky
Knowing that she's really her
When she doesn't have to try

How I love her
So very much

'Feelings like ours
only come together
once in a lifetime

there aren't any second chances'

OUR LOVE IS STRONGER THAN ANYTHING

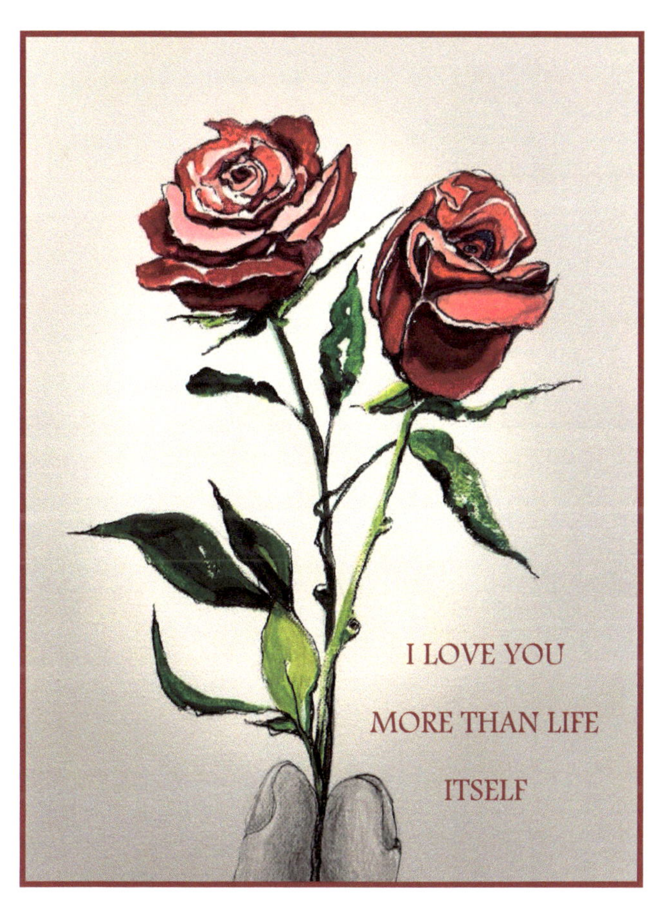

I LOVE YOU

MORE THAN LIFE

ITSELF

NANCY NANCY

nancy nancy nancy nancy nancy nancy nancy love
nancy nancy nancy nancy nancy nancy nancy nanc
love nancy nancy nancy nancy nancy nancy nanc
nancy nancy love nancy nancy nancy nancy nanc
nancy nancy love nancy nancy nancy love nancy na
nancy nancy nancy nancy nancy nancy nancy love
nancy nancy nancy nancy nancy nancy nancy nanc
love nancy nancy nancy nancy nancy nancy nanc
nancy nancy love nancy nancy nancy nancy nanc
nancy nancy nancy nancy nancy nancy nancy love

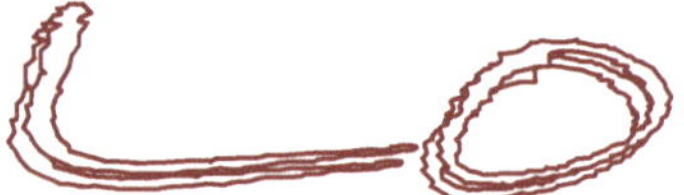

LOVE NANCY

ncy nancy nancy nancy nancy nancy nancy nancy
ancy nancy nancy nancy nancy nancy nancy nancy
ancy nancy nancy love nancy nancy nancy nancy
ancy nancy love nancy nancy nancy nancy nancy
 nancy nancy nancy love nancy nancy nancy nancy
ncy nancy nancy nancy nancy nancy nancy nancy
ancy nancy nancy nancy nancy nancy nancy nancy
ancy nancy nancy love nancy nancy nancy nancy
ancy nancy love nancy nancy nancy nancy nancy
ncy nancy nancy nancy nancy nancy nancy nancy

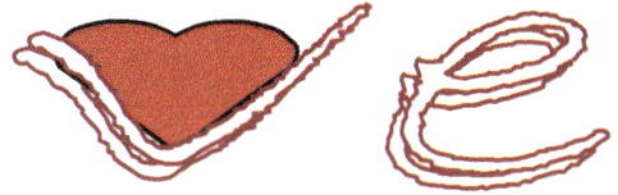

'I have no doubts about us

we are too much alike'

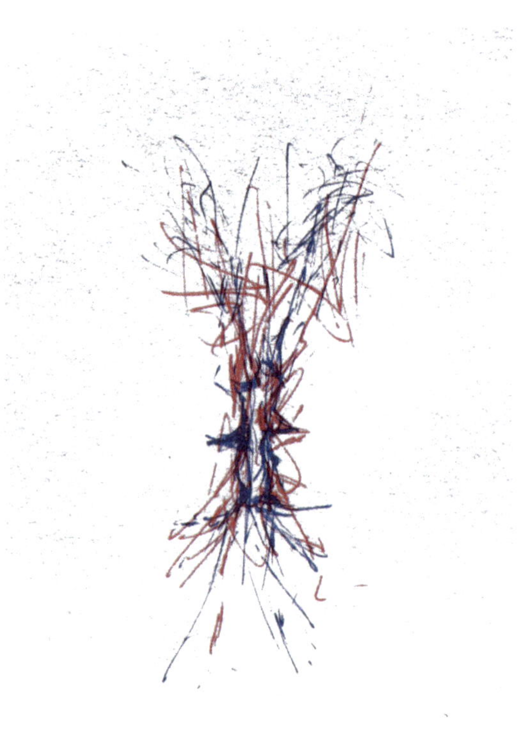

15

TRILOGY in 4 Verses

Mountains
There's always mountains to climb
some are very high
some reach to the sky
but I tell you something
I'm going to climb this one

Sunshine
There goes my sunshine
to be caught but once a day
then lost within a shadow
on a grey-top floating cloud
there goes my sunshine
passing by my frosted window
isn't ever day I see her
but when I do I know

My Love
She's always there
with loving touch and gentle care
she is she is my love
and nothing comes before my love
not even me

Forever More
This may be the last time I see you
or it may be forever more
it's now, up to you
to decide, to make me sure

'With love there

most of your problems are solved before you start

because love always comes first'

Across the oceans

Across the oceans
You can see for miles
Beyond the eye of man

A place so far away
That no other can

And when you wish upon a star
You know that you will be
Chasing shadows effortlessly
Across the cyan sea

'I too wish
we had spent more time together'

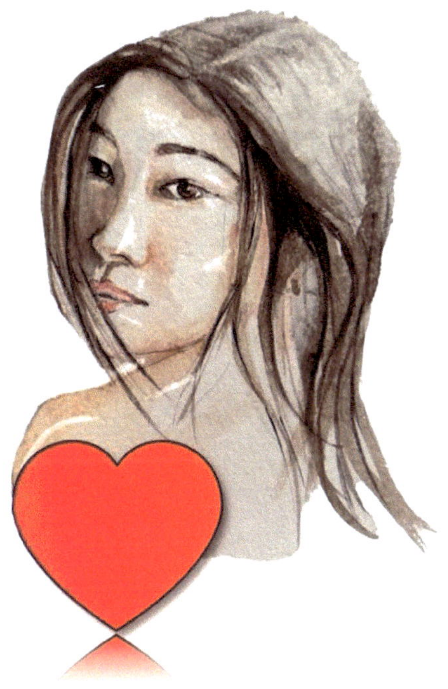

'This is a most important time
perhaps the most important time
of our lives......

and I intend to be with you
so that we can work it out
together......'

'At certain moments
in your life
you are just lost for words'

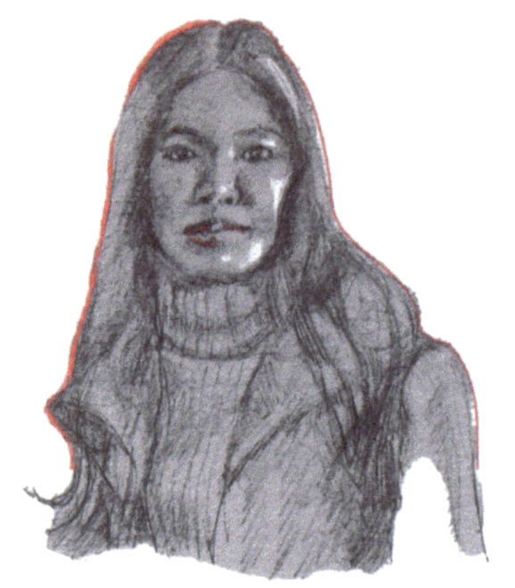

'I think it's really true

there are no words for love

It's feeling and knowing

and never having to ask 'why'

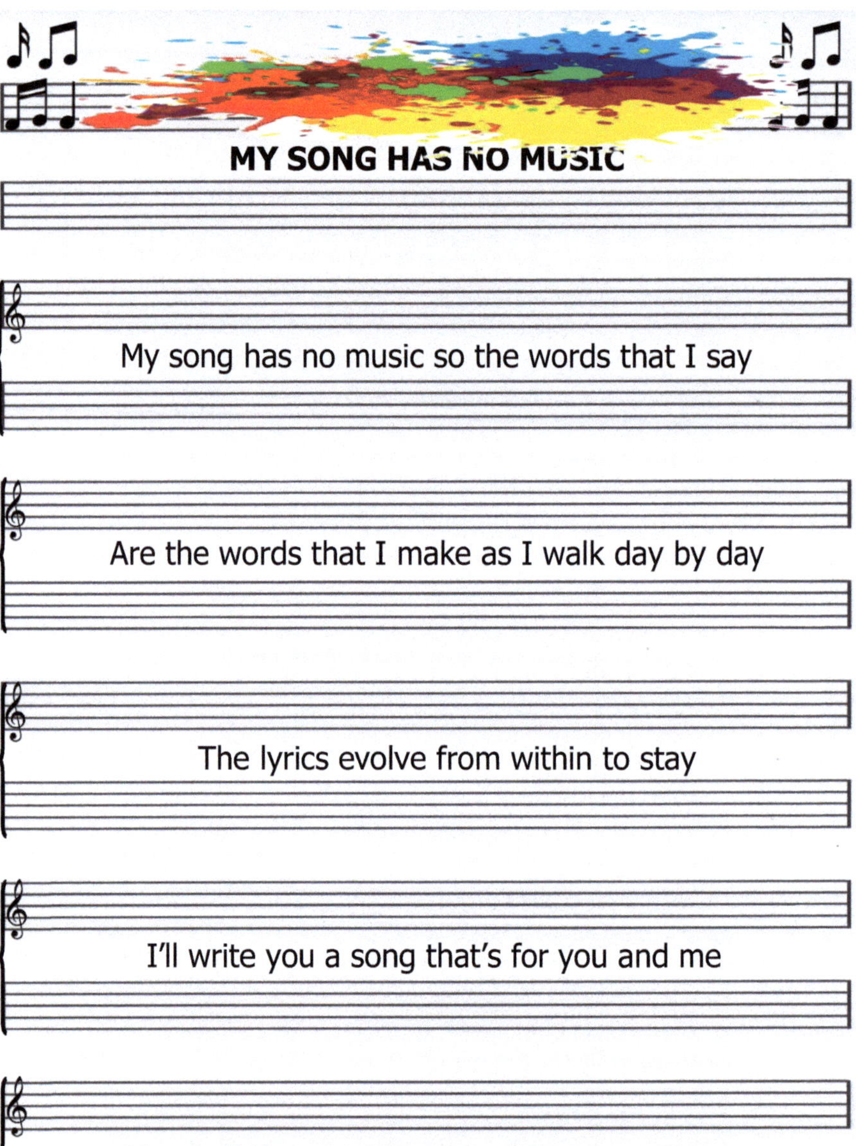

MY SONG HAS NO MUSIC

My song has no music so the words that I say

Are the words that I make as I walk day by day

The lyrics evolve from within to stay

I'll write you a song that's for you and me

About all the good times and the way we agree

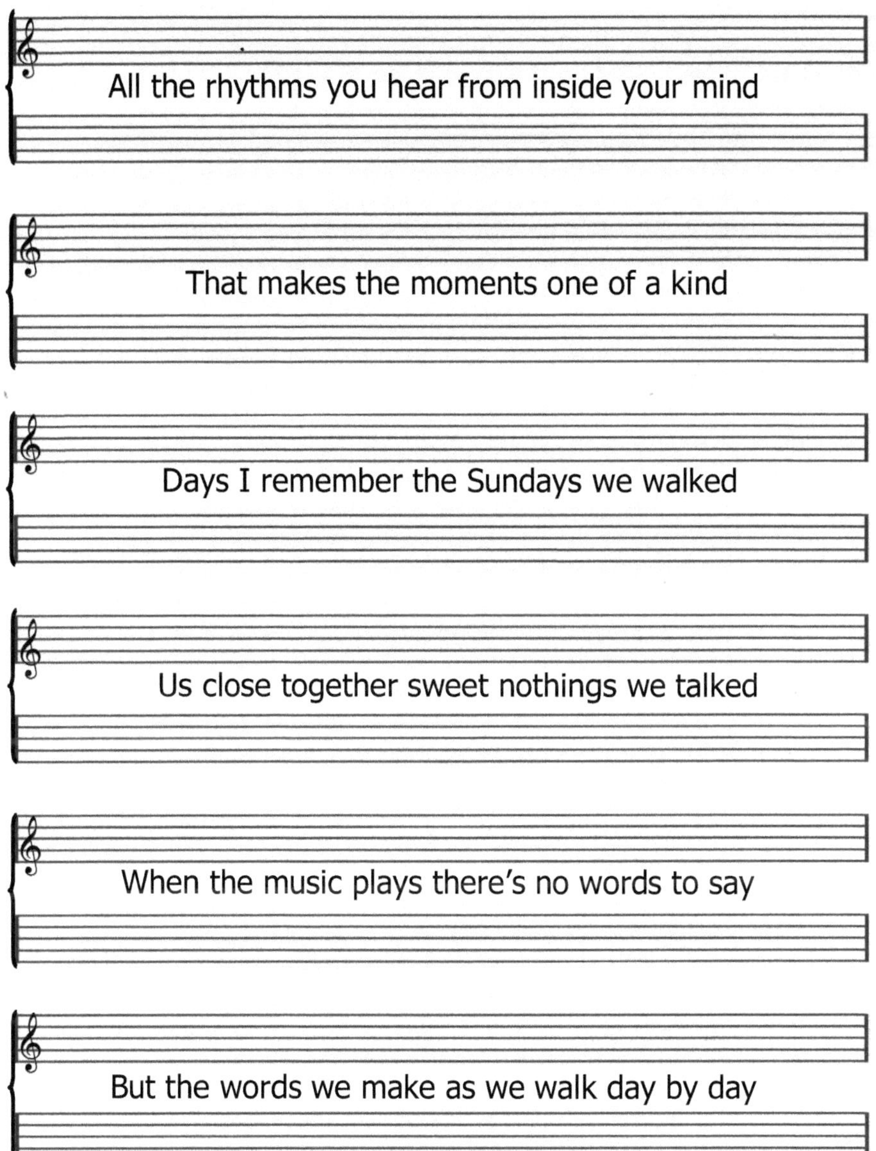

All the rhythms you hear from inside your mind
That makes the moments one of a kind
Days I remember the Sundays we walked
Us close together sweet nothings we talked
When the music plays there's no words to say
But the words we make as we walk day by day

'True love grows
It grows on you
Budding, like the leaves of a tree
And when it's there
You both really know
When the tree starts to grow
It becomes every part of your body
And you are as one

And nothing can take it away'

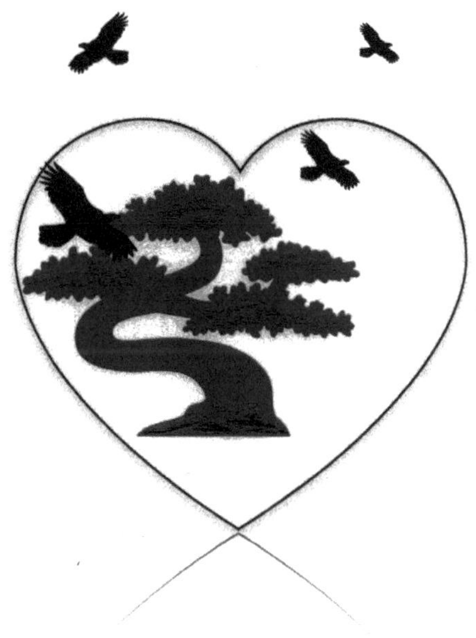

'Some people never find love

We are lucky

For I am sure we have'

LOVE YOU, YOU

I love you, you
love you, love you, love you

and I'll keep on saying so
'til the day you say
I know you do

YOU

You are you
as you are who you are
that's why I love you so

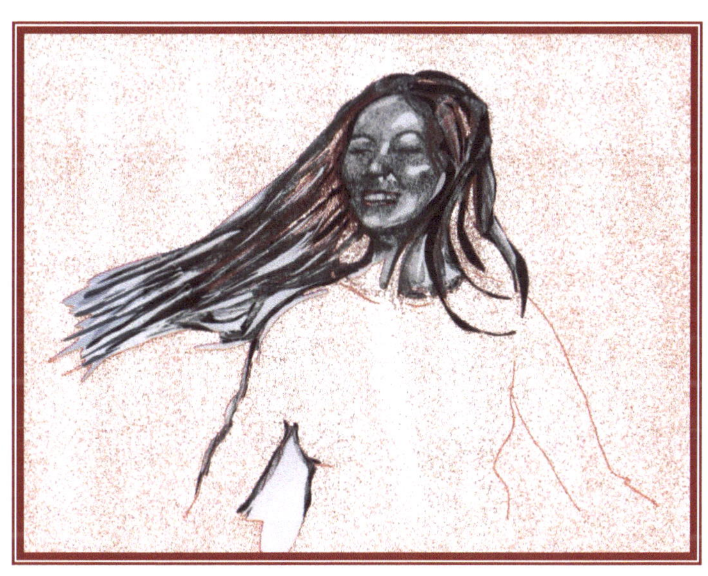

'It's what you are to me
I know I love you more than life
As I will always truly love you

    I have never felt this love for anyone before'

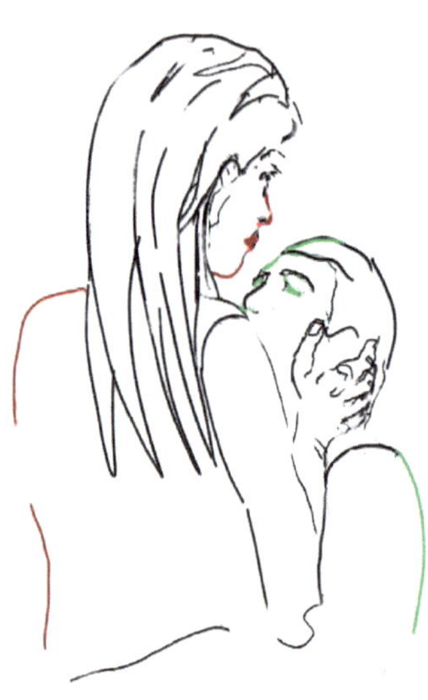

You're All

You're all that love is made of
You're all the petal flowers
You're all the dream made hours

all the silver moons
            all the sunshine tunes
    all the lilac trees
                all the sweetest breeze
        all the skies of gold
            all the fortunes told
all the ocean sands
all the wonderlands
        all the milky ways
            all the warmest days

You're all I ever see
            you're everything to me

HOW WONDERFUL IF

COULD HAVE A STRONGER

FOR THEY WOULD THEN BE ABLE

MORE PEOPLE IN THE WORLD

BELIEF IN THEIR OWN FEELINGS

TO UNDERSTAND THEMSELVES BETTER

'That's a lovely picture on the card you sent
We must go there when I come
I have never met anyone like you either
I could not have written like that
to anyone else
You are everything to me
How I miss you
Your happiness will always be my happiness
I love you so
Thinking of you every moment
'til we are together
I will make you happy
in every way I know how
We are too much the same
You are everything to me
I know you must believe this now
Hope you had a happy birthday darling
It is always with my constant love that I write
How I long to be with you
Let it be soon for both of us
Shall be counting the days
When we shall be together again'

FLY WITH MY WORDS

There are Things

There are things I want to do for you
If you'll only let me decide for you
there are worlds I want to make for you
If you'll only let me create as two
There are places I want to take you to
If only you'll let me walk with you
There are things I want to buy for you
If you'll only let me try for you
There is love I want to give to you
If you'll only let me love you too

'I am looking forward to saying hello to your
parents

I leave it to you
to let me know the right moment'

I know I can rely on your judgement'

'I hope you can always confide in me
for I shall always want to be able
to talk things over
                    and advise you for the best

As I shall turn to you in the future
                    and ask of your advice'

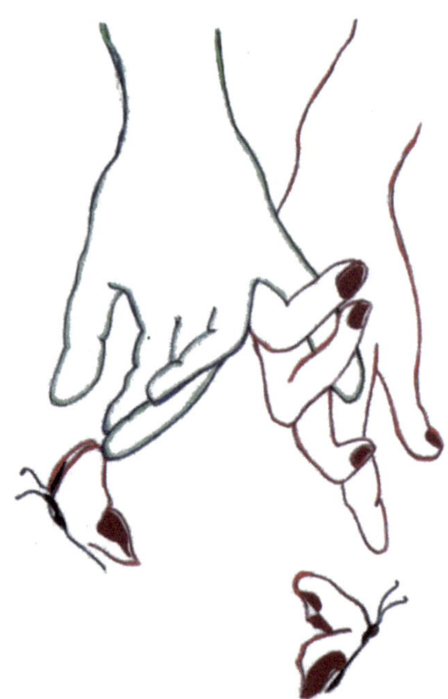

Turn To Each Other

We talk about our problems
Like Father, Mother, Sister, Brother
Talk about our problems
Sit down and work things out
We know we are the same
In the many of our ways
There is no other
Things will always turn out fine
Will do, all down the line
With our love watch it grow
For we can always turn to each other
And this is the only way to know

'There is that special something
between us

It could only be fate
that bought us together'

我老欢喜侬个。

WOH~HUN~SEE~NEE

I LOVE YOU VERY MUCH

If (one verse)

If I had searched a lifetime
I could never find another you
If the stars and fate
Be all they are
Then I know
They must be true

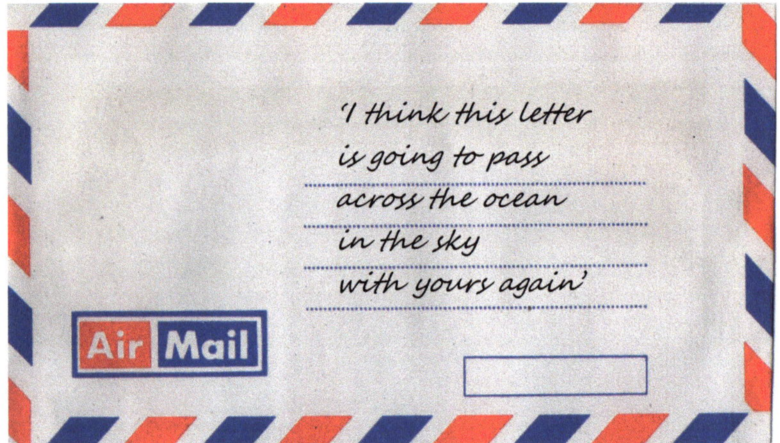

'I think this letter
is going to pass
across the ocean
in the sky
with yours again'

Air Mail

If I could Find The Words

If I could find the words to say
I'd write you letters every day
I'd send you gifts by twenty score
Each day, I'd send you more and more
I'd travel all the roads there are
Across the world both near and far
I'd tell you all the things I'd do
How every moment, I think of you
With all the love I've found
Just by knowing you're around
Everything you've done for me
Just by being who you be

'I shall always feel the same love for you

For such a love is an undying love'

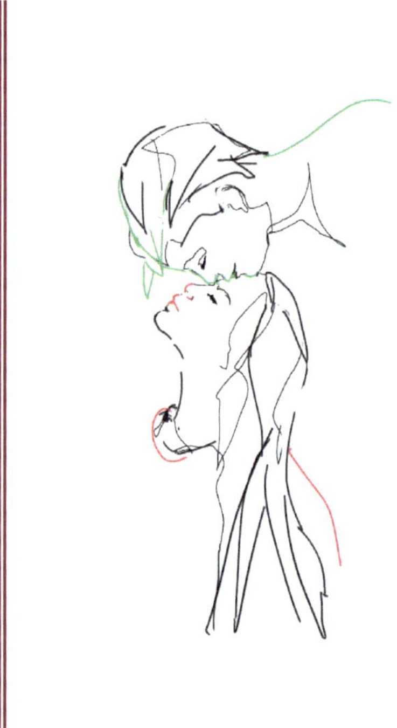

'These are not words of the moment darling

They are for ever'

If Forever

If forever is forever
To have you near to me
Then that's how I want it be

If forever is forever
To kiss your lips of wine
Then I'll not decline

If forever is forever
You and me on every moon
Then it will never come too soon

If forever is forever
Smiling girls and boys
Then I'll buy them all their toys

If forever is forever
To love you all I can
Then there's nothing better than

If forever is forever
My life through with you
Then that's all I want to do

Then that's all I want to do

Then that's all I want to do

I hope we are truthful with each other
and with ourselves

For if we are
we shall always be happy together

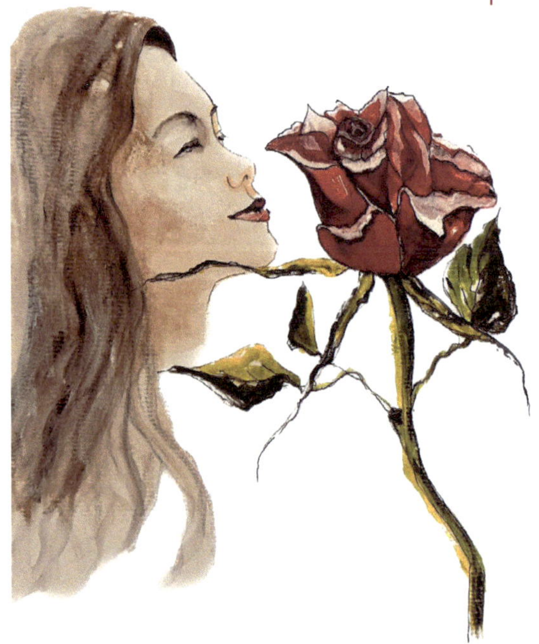

One Day

One day I'll ask you
Look into my eyes
Don't tell me lies
I won't run and cry
I won't say goodbye
You only have to tell me
You don't have to sell me
I know you and you know me
And old Father Time
Well, he can see

'You are my love, my only love
There could never be another

         I know this as I know myself '

'I so look forward to being near you again

            and have your arms around me'

47

My Love

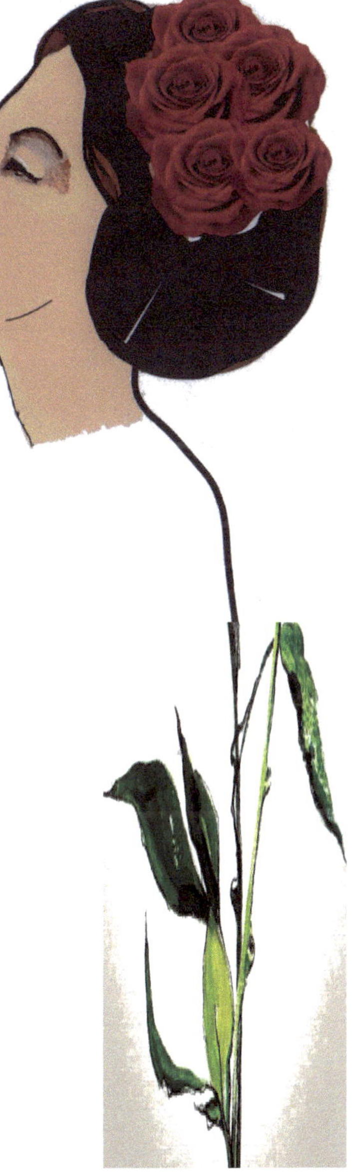

I know my love
is my only love

My feelings greater than
than I ever can

She's all my dreams
and golden scenes

All the things
the love ring brings

She's everyone to me
though one she only be

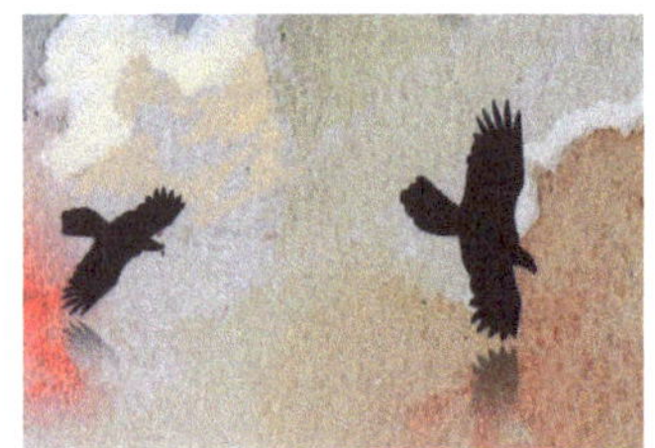

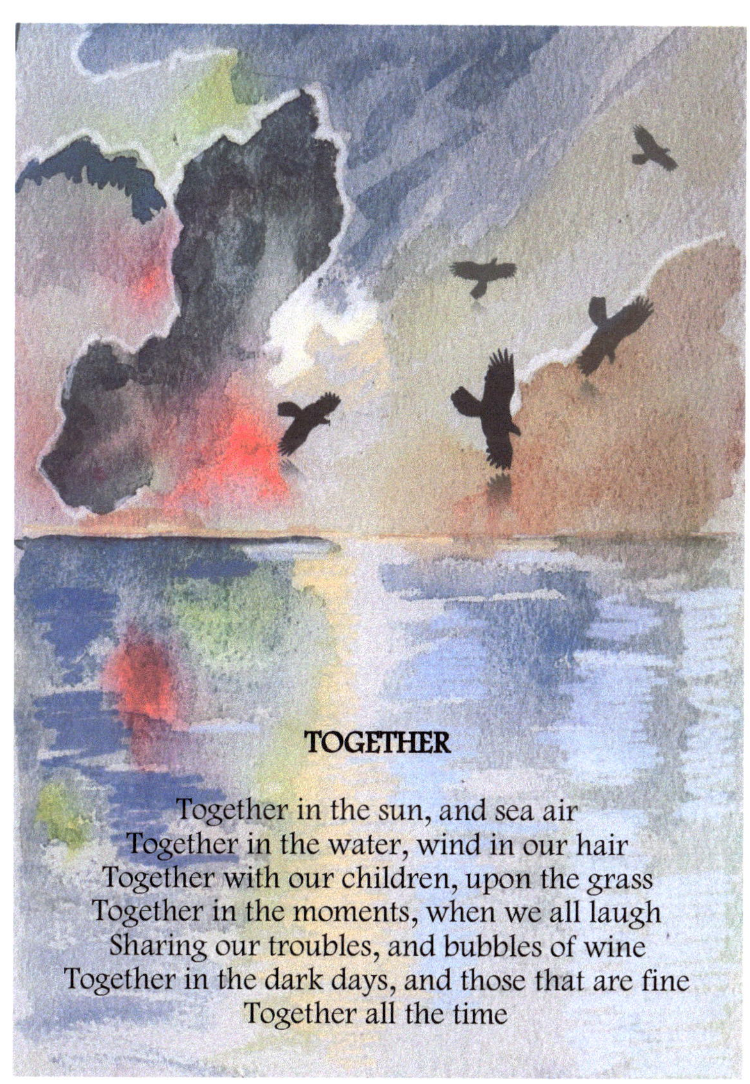

TOGETHER

Together in the sun, and sea air
Together in the water, wind in our hair
Together with our children, upon the grass
Together in the moments, when we all laugh
Sharing our troubles, and bubbles of wine
Together in the dark days, and those that are fine
Together all the time

'no, I don't think you are shy
just very feminine

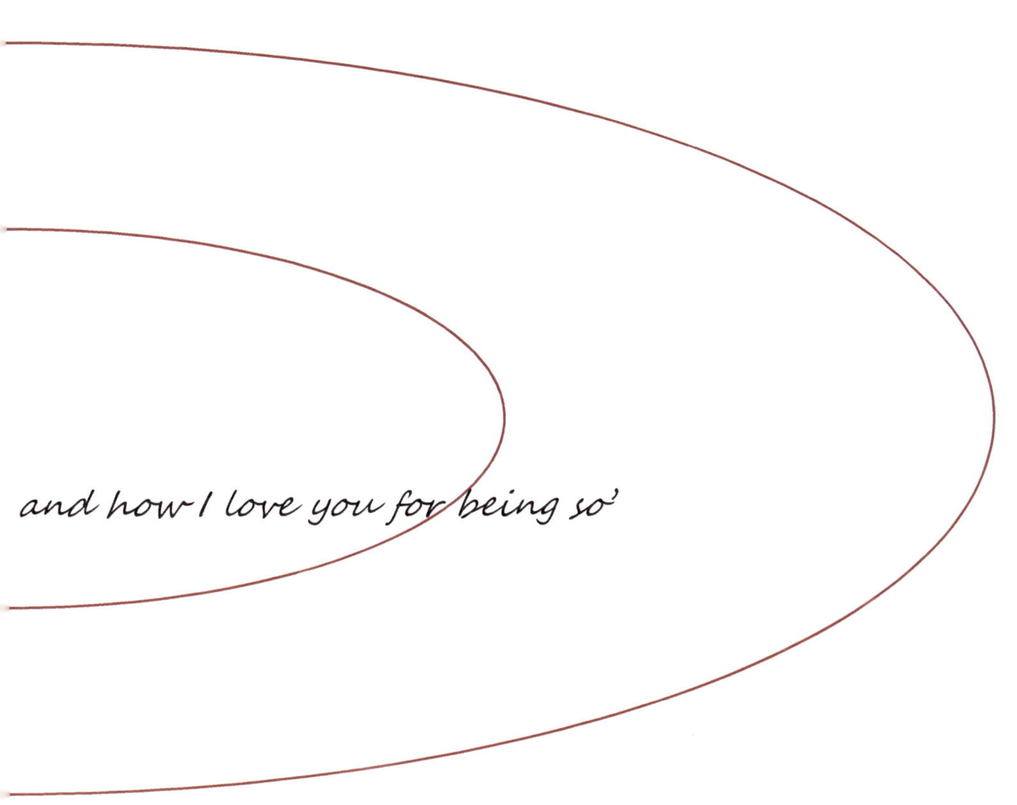
and how I love you for being so'

<h1 style="text-align:center">…..**More than**……</h1>

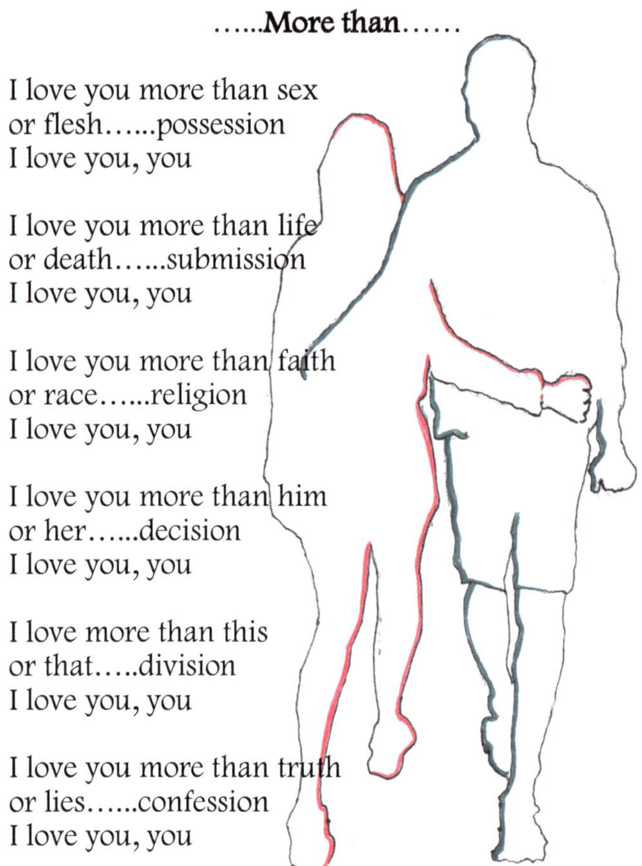

I love you more than sex
or flesh…...possession
I love you, you

I love you more than life
or death…...submission
I love you, you

I love you more than faith
or race…...religion
I love you, you

I love you more than him
or her…...decision
I love you, you

I love more than this
or that…..division
I love you, you

I love you more than truth
or lies…...confession
I love you, you

'you are everything in a women
I have ever hoped to find

You are the maker
of my mind'

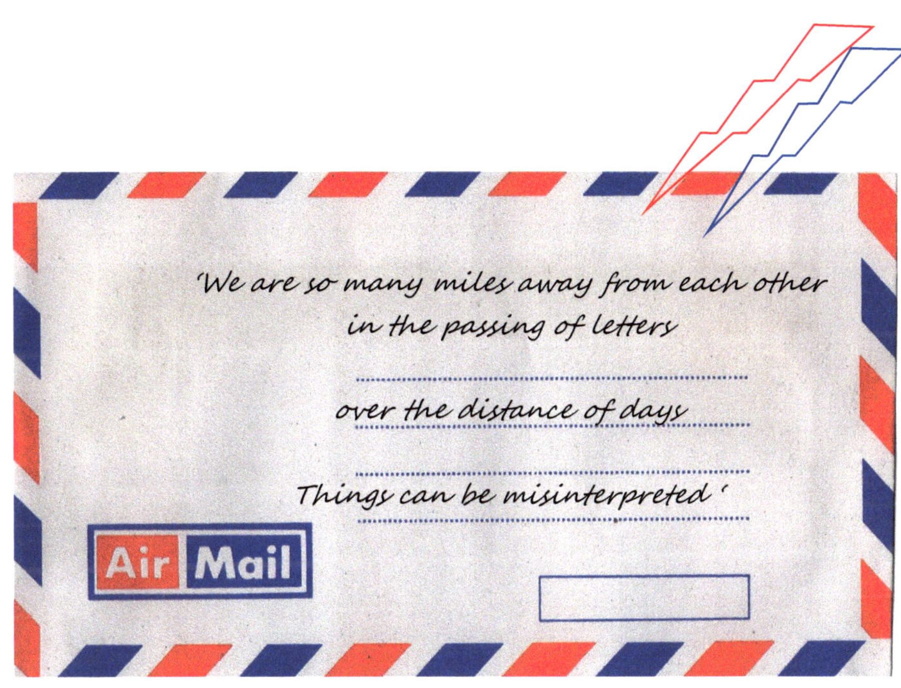
'We are so many miles away from each other
in the passing of letters

over the distance of days

Things can be misinterpreted '

Air Mail

ARE WE LOST
ARE WE NOT
LET'S MAKE A DECISION
BEFORE WE TRAVEL
TO THE LAND
THAT TIME FORGOT

Are We

Are we understanding each other
Are we thinking how and why our ways
Are we pulling closer together
Could it take a few more days

Are we saying all we feel
Are we believing what is real

Could we be complicating thoughts
Ringing with the liberty bell
Then in time
Our love will tell

'you know that anything I do for you
Is because I love you with all my heart'...............

For You…....

I'll do anything for you

I'll do all I should for you
I'll walk on water for you
I'll solve your troubles for you
I'll blow a bubble for you

I'll do anything for you

I'll chase time for you
I'll make it fine for you
I'll make it glow for you
I'll stage a show for you

I'll do anything for you

I'll go to mars for you
I'll gather stars for you
I'll walk in space for you
I'll fly with grace for you

I'll do anything for you
I'll do anything for you

I love you for all you are

          exactly as you are

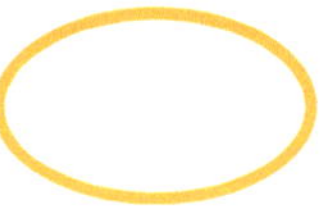

All I ever wish for

    is to spend my whole life through with you

Beyond You

Beyond you
There's a sky of gold
There's stars to unfold
There's a forgotten sea
There's many silver moons
There's sunshine silken tunes
All the musical balloons
Beyond you
There's reality
      reality
        reality
          reality
        reality
     reality
  reality

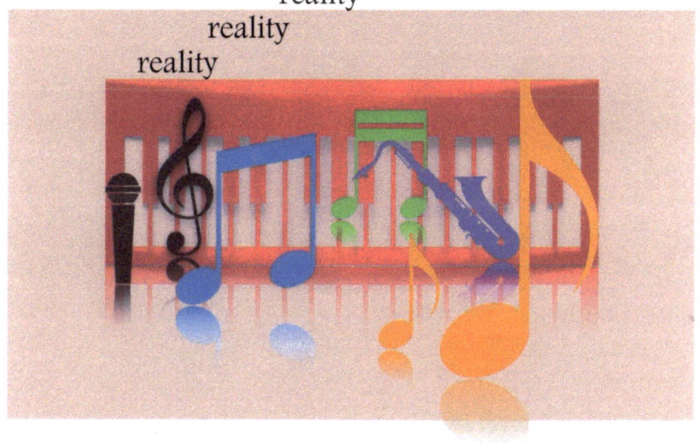

How

How do you know
when you are in love
before you love

then I know not what love is

How do you know
when you are in love
before you love

then I know not what love is

How do you know
when you are in love
before you love

But, I now know what love is

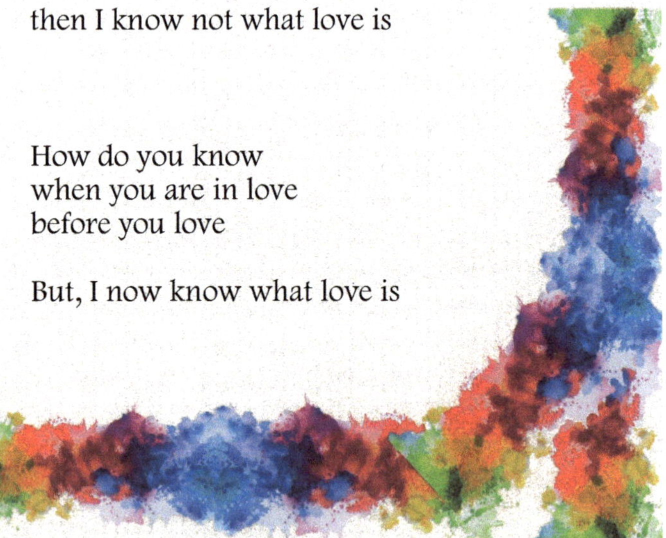

As I read your letters
I feel your nearness each time

Only two days have passed
since your last letter
and it already seems like months

I have known a number of girls over the years
Some I have felt affection for.................................

............but with none have I ever had the feeling
I have with you

ON a BED of ROSES

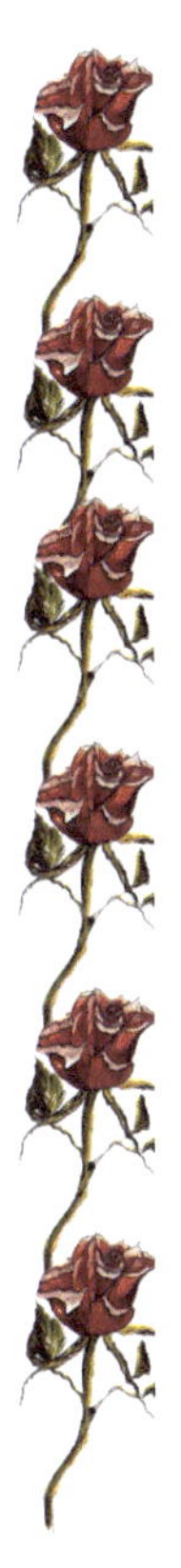

On a bed of roses as you lie
looking up to open sky
filled with passion in your mind
your body starts today unwind
growing up and out inside
your muscles tract and sub-divide
the slightest movement in your eye
beckons forth deepest cry
that hottest moment instant comes
beating out like jungle drums
taking all your strength within
swimming round the ocean rim
control is lost forever gone
like a symphony of song
as heaven opens up its door
forever wanting more and more

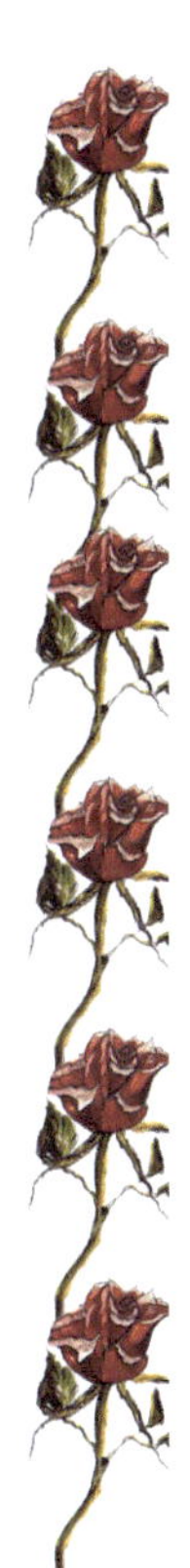

If there could be any change
                                    It would only be that
I love you more and more over the years

                                    Love can only grow
       with the love I have for you

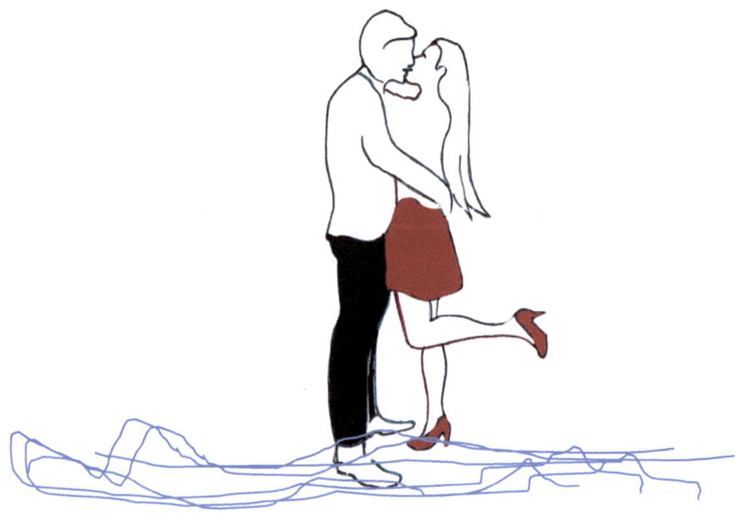

So In Love

I'm so in love
I don't see the sky any more
I'm so in love
I don't see the ocean shore
Creep between my toes
As I walk and daydream beneath the stars

AND hell, what do I care
What people think of me
They may say I'm in a trance
That this is my last chance
To spend a freedom life

Well what about the days ahead
If you haven't got a wife
When all is said and done
What about the children
If you're the only one

I believe you only meet one person in your life that
you really love

                and darling I've met you

                        I also believe
                        There is an outward love
                        and an inward love

                                I know my love for you
                                Is a very deep inward love

I could ask no more of life
Than for you to have the same love for me

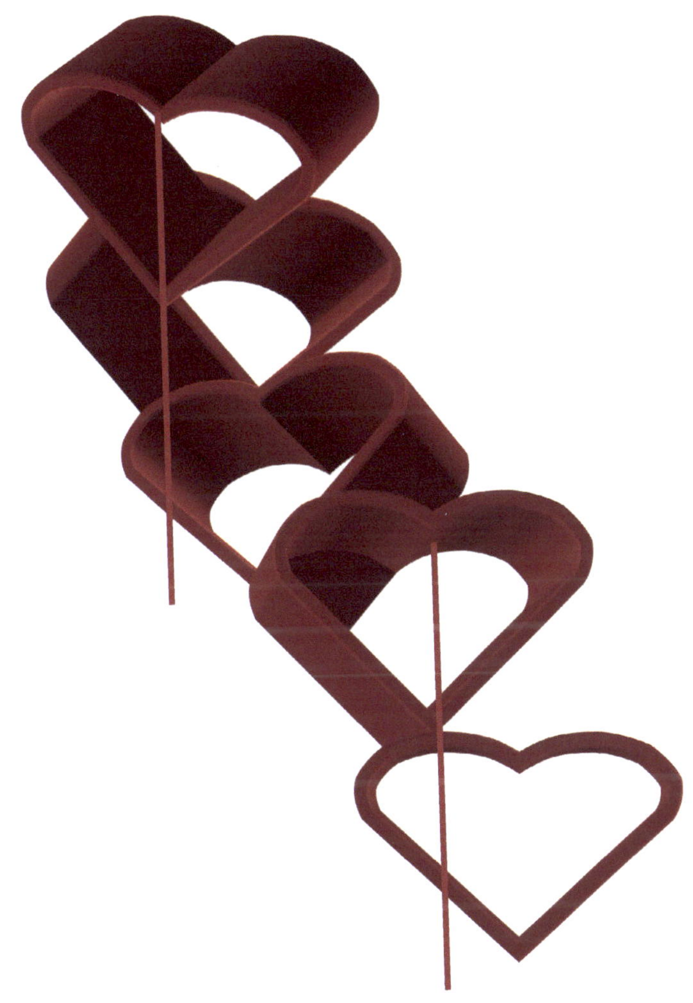

Finding Love *(February '72)*

How the moments passed
how they passed so fast
we sat hands across the table
as though across the sea
looking into each others eyes
as we drank our Irish coffee

And after, as it grew dark
and we were asked to leave the park
how the minutes flew by
past the midnight sky
we sat and talked for hours
about our future life
of us together, man and wife

When I look back again
on the morning you caught the plane
how a million moments filled me inside
but not a word could I find
as you put your arms around me
and kissed me your goodbye
although, you know somehow
a tear, but nearly filled my eye

We found love that night
in the early hours of the dawn

Perhaps at the moment
My love is stronger for you
Than you for me

It is enough that you say 'I love you'

This is a giant step we boththth taketaketake
We 're talking about aboutour whole life through

Each Day By Day

are you sure
am I sure
in everything we say
are there doubts and queries
in the wonder of our words
each day by day

have you found
have I found
certain feelings go astray
as we think each new thought
each day by day

do you know
do I know
as we go along the way
in the footsteps that we take
each day by day

are we sure
so sure we're sure
in everything we say
with no doubts or queries
in the wonder of our words
each day by day

When we see each other
it will all be our emotions running through......

.......the electricity there is between us
that makes us so much the same

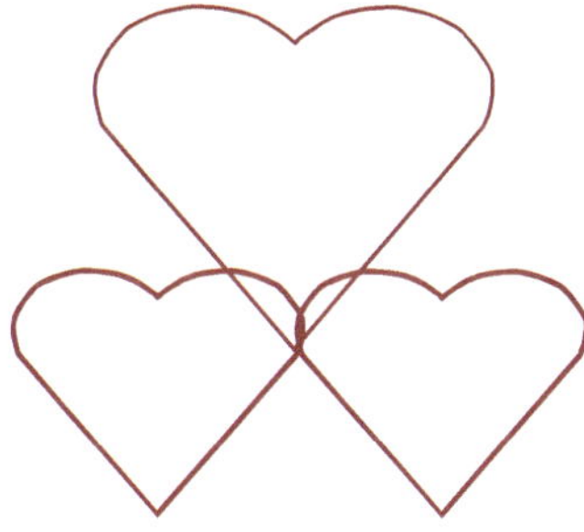

Waiting

Waiting
Riding on a moon so blue

Waiting
Floating on a sea of lilac

Waiting
Feeling starlight closer to

Waiting
For the day you come back

Waiting
For you for you

How I remember the first time we met
I felt I 'd known you a lifetime before

Many Love Songs

Many love songs have I sung
Many love letters have I begun
But the letters I remember most
Are the letters I wrote to you

Many love tales have I heard
Many told with untrue word
But the tales I know are true
Are the tales they tell of you

Many love words I have written
Many words that I am smitten
But the words I remember most
Are the words I wrote to you

Many love days have gone past
Many times have we laughed
But the days I laughed the most
Are the days I laughed with you

Many lovers I have had
As many good as many bad
But the love I remember most
Is the love I share with you

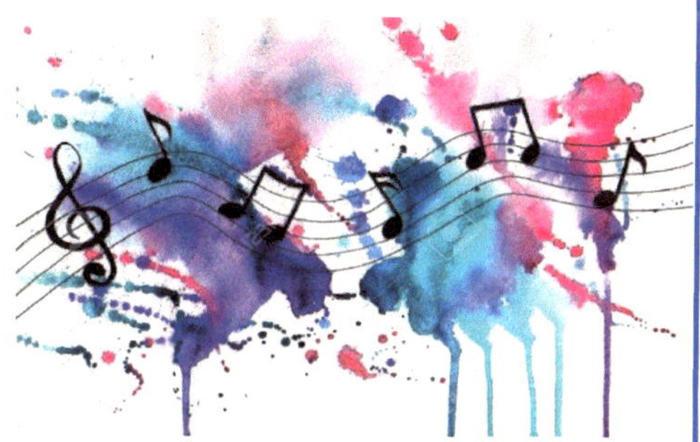

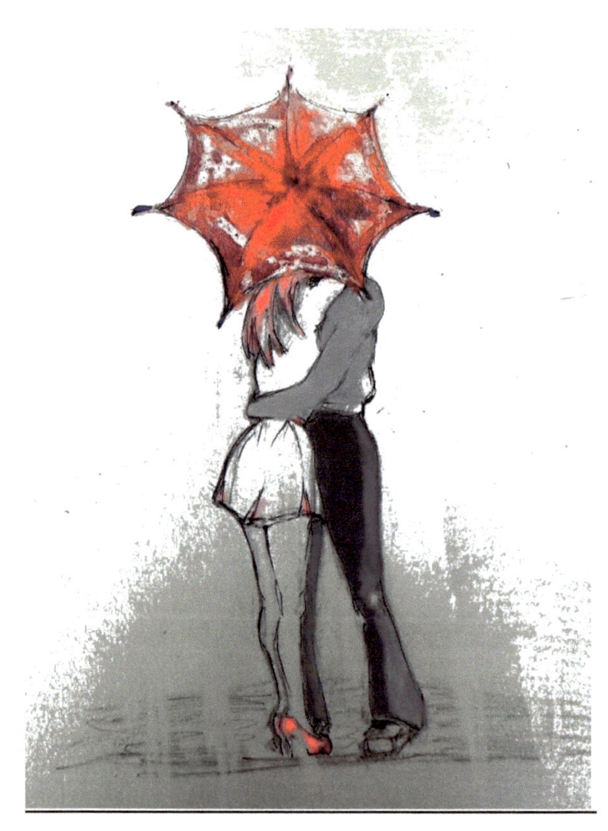

There was that special something
from the very beginning

Many Love Days

Many love days have I wept
Many nights I never slept
But the nights I wept the most
Are the nights I wept for you

Many wishes have I wished
Many times have I been kissed
But the kisses I remember most
Are the kisses I had with you

Many women have I met
Many that I now forget
But no woman was the one
'till the day that I met you

Many people have I known
Many small and now tall grown
But the one I remember most
Is the face I see of you

Many travels have I made
Many moments often fade
But the moment I remember most
Is the moment I met you

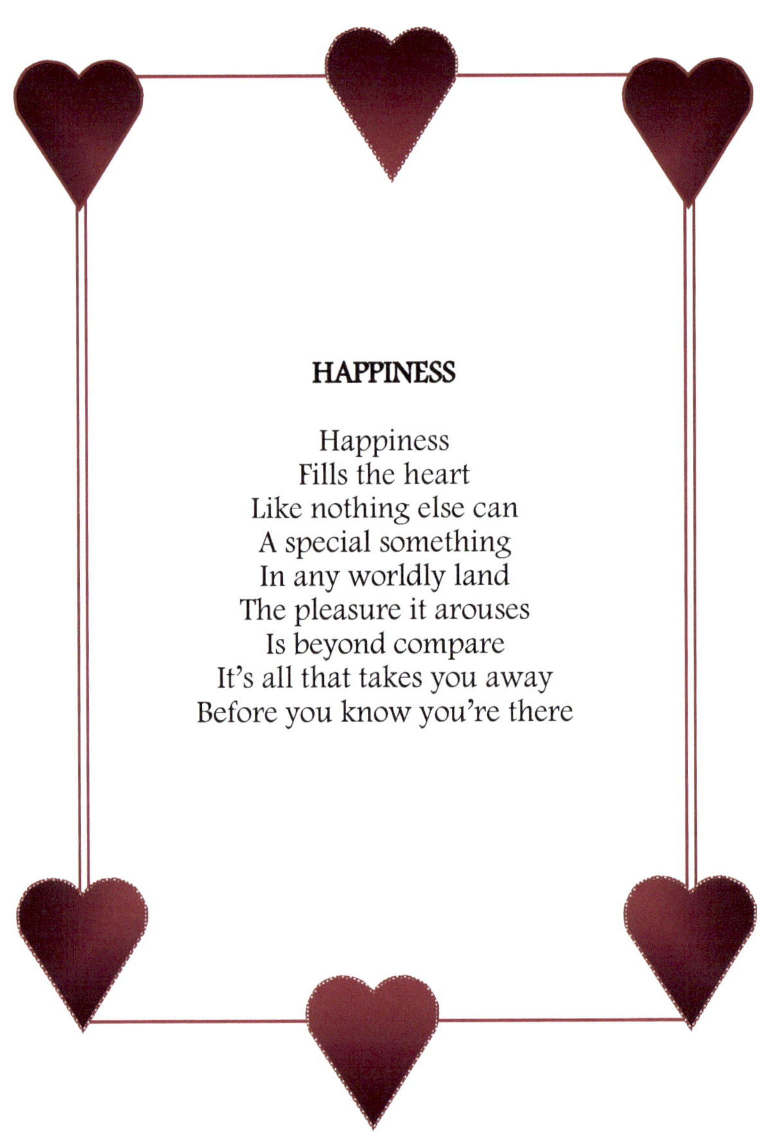

HAPPINESS

Happiness
Fills the heart
Like nothing else can
A special something
In any worldly land
The pleasure it arouses
Is beyond compare
It's all that takes you away
Before you know you're there

How lucky we are to have found each other

I know we'll be happy throughout our life

For you cannot buy happiness

It's there between you

As it shall always be with us

I remember_________

When I first met your Father

He asked me________

'Do you love my daughter'

I replied_________

'I do, with all my heart'

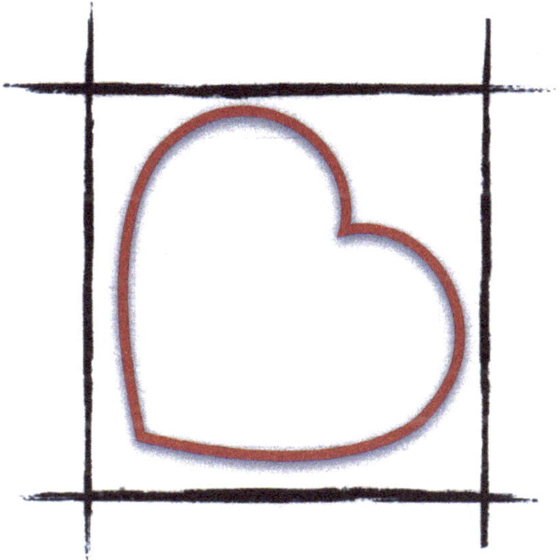

Wherever I am
        I would always want you with me
        I don't want to spend any days without you
        I love you too much

Being with You

Being with you
you just being
makes all my seeing be true
before I lived in wonder
days of quiet nights
just listening to the thunder
but now I have a name to turn to

Across my shoulder over yonder
I know there will be you

Always

I'll always love you
with all the love anyone can give
I'll always think of you
every moment that I live

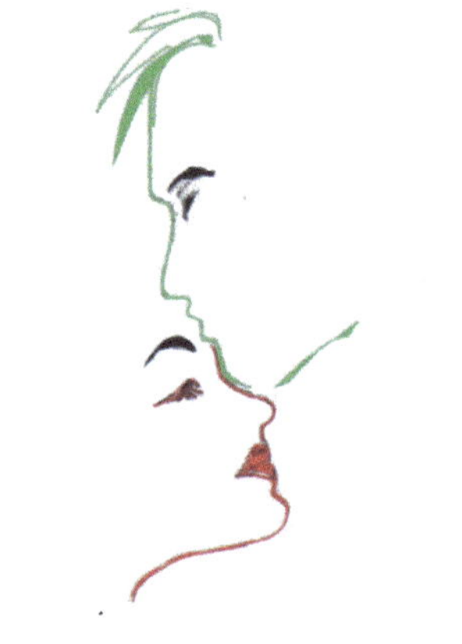

Time will fly
and we shall be in each others arms again
sharing our kisses

How I love you

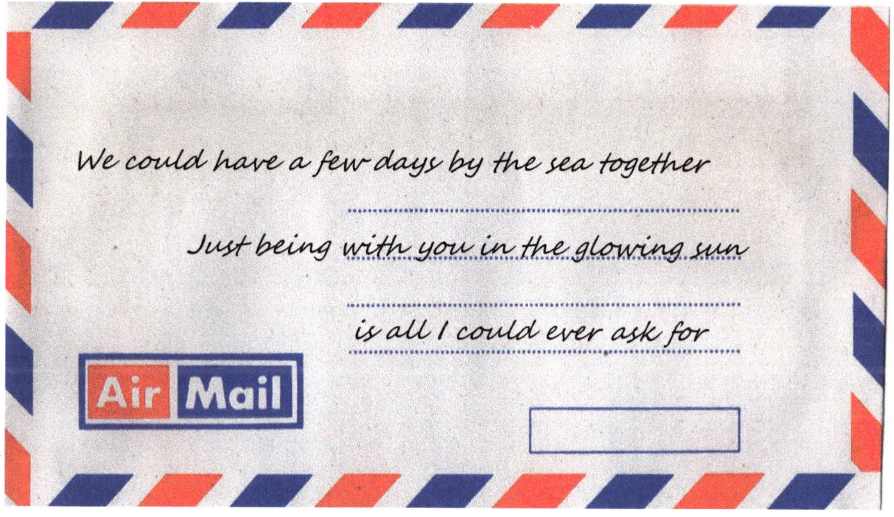

We could have a few days by the sea together

Just being with you in the glowing sun

is all I could ever ask for

Air Mail

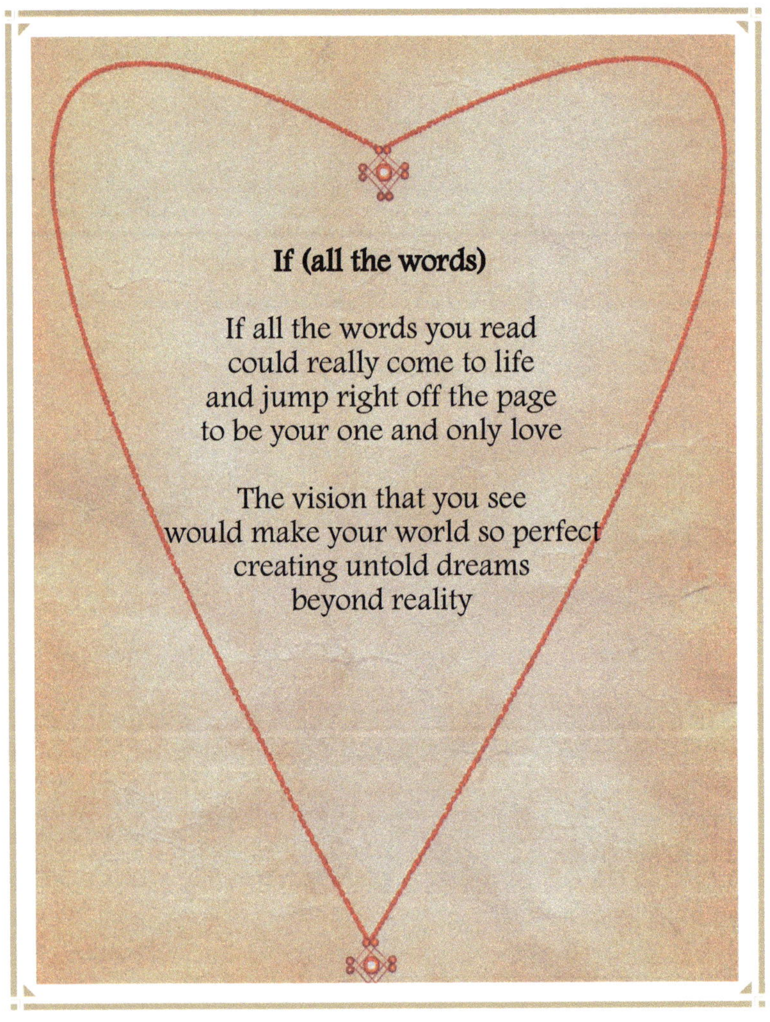

If (all the words)

If all the words you read
could really come to life
and jump right off the page
to be your one and only love

The vision that you see
would make your world so perfect
creating untold dreams
beyond reality

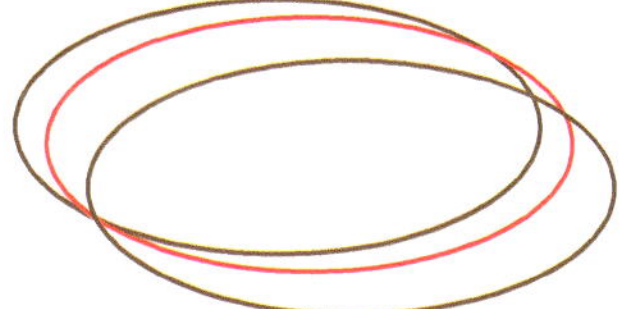

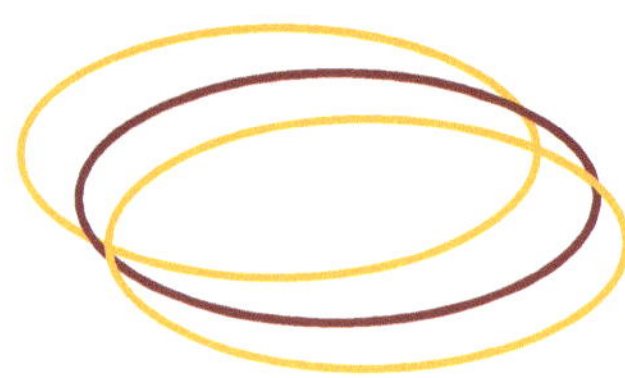

I'm sure we shall share unforgettable moments
with the golden sun glowing down on us
above the sea breeze

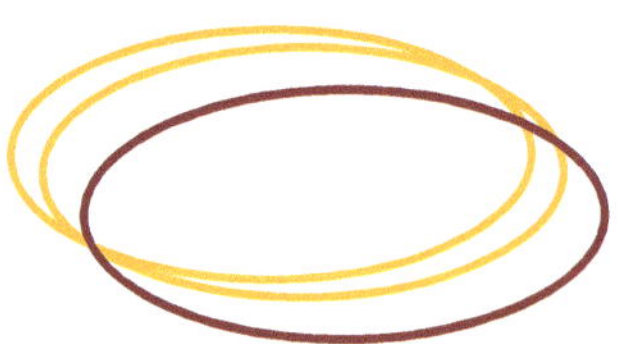

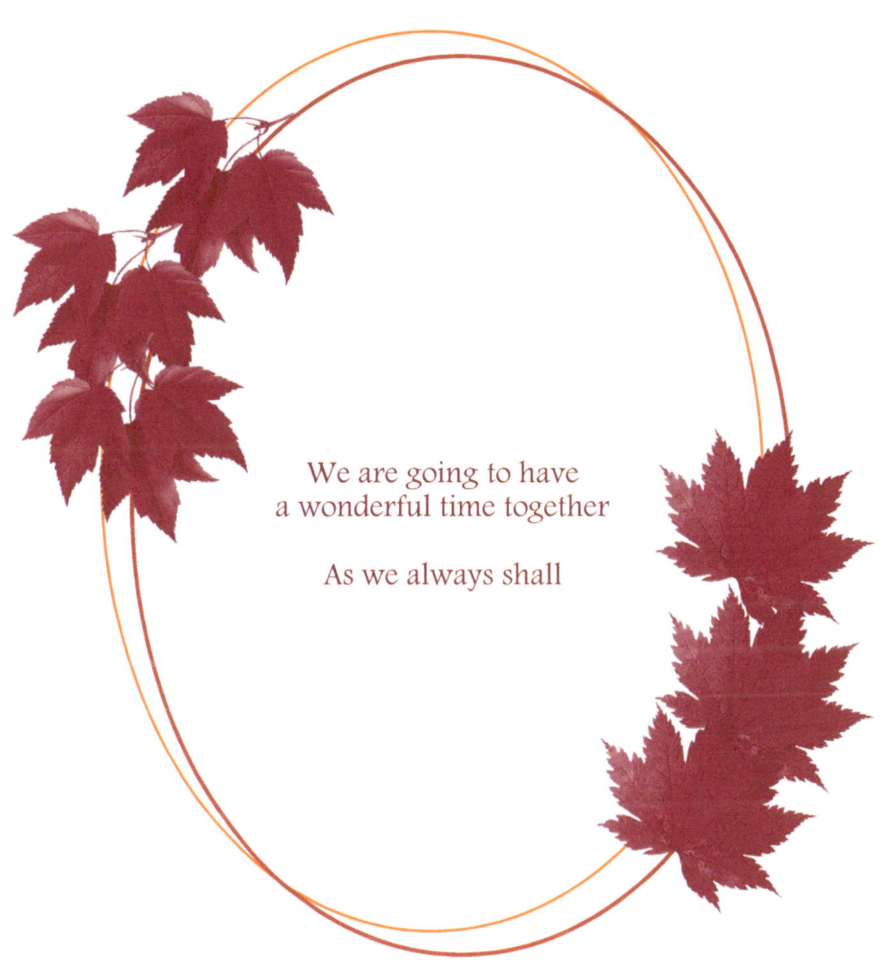

We are going to have
a wonderful time together

As we always shall

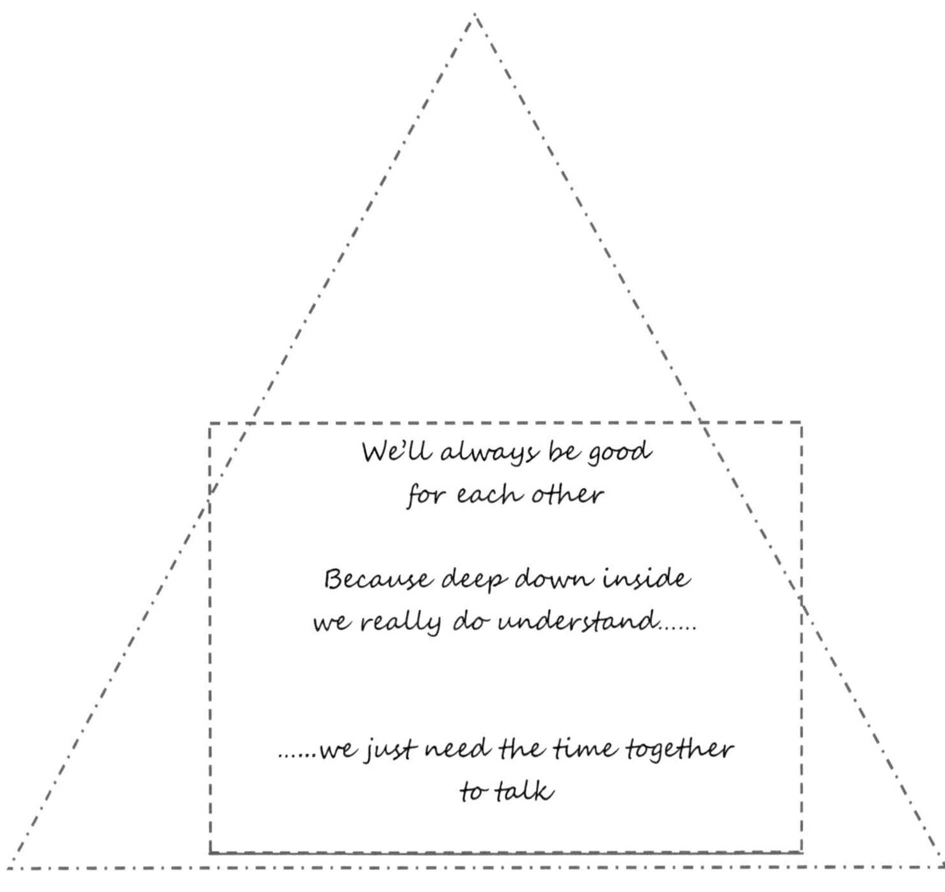

We'll always be good
for each other

Because deep down inside
we really do understand......

......we just need the time together
to talk

Since Ancient Days

In all the world
Since ancient days
The word of love
Is a certainty
Still holds the key
To all eternity

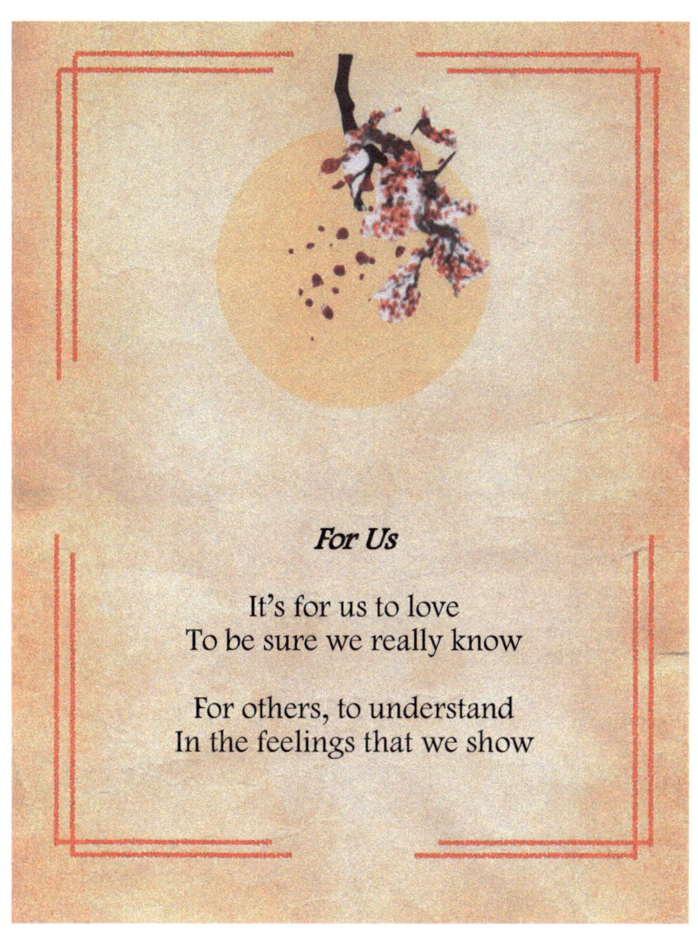

For Us

It's for us to love
To be sure we really know

For others, to understand
In the feelings that we show

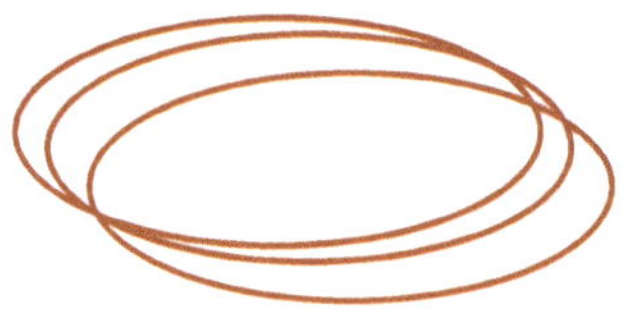

It's the electricity between us
that makes us so much the same

You' are
everything in a woman
I've ever dreamed of

I love you so very much

97

Every Step

You are every step I take
Every word I make
All the stars that glow
In the deep blue galactic sky
The one and only being
That tells me I'll get by
You who sealed my soul with love
Held tight in a golden glove

As we ran across
The green green hills
The world stood still
With a million thrills
Each day was forever new
As time but flew

What I do know
For a certainty
We shall always be
From Here To Eternity

Because we've been apart for so many weeks
we may be a little on edge toward each other
I think it's because we miss each other so much

GOODBYE HELLO

Goodbye hello
Start again, stop and go
Hello goodbye
Not for good, so don't cry
Will miss you so
Please don't go
Hello hello

Wave your hand as we go
How long 'til when
I don't know
Tell me soon
And make it so
Hello hello

Work out problems
In our mind
Won't be long
'til I find
That you know
I love you so
Hello hello

      hello hello

        hello

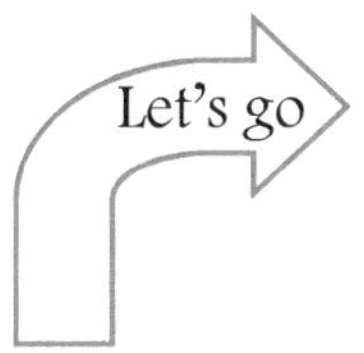

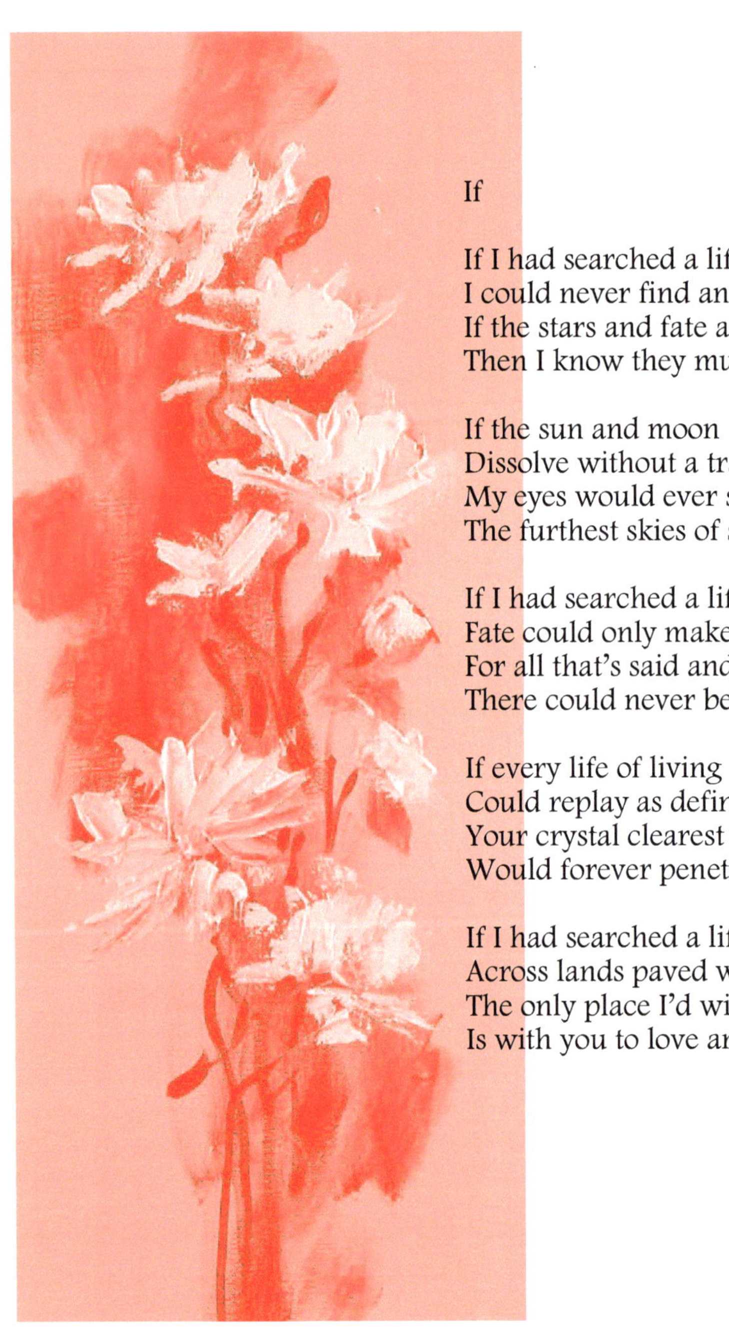

If

If I had searched a lifetime
I could never find another you
If the stars and fate are all they are
Then I know they must be true

If the sun and moon
Dissolve without a trace
My eyes would ever see beyond
The furthest skies of space

If I had searched a lifetime
Fate could only make it true
For all that's said and done
There could never be another you

If every life of living
Could replay as defined
Your crystal clearest image
Would forever penetrate my mind

If I had searched a lifetime
Across lands paved with gold
The only place I'd wish to be
Is with you to love and hold

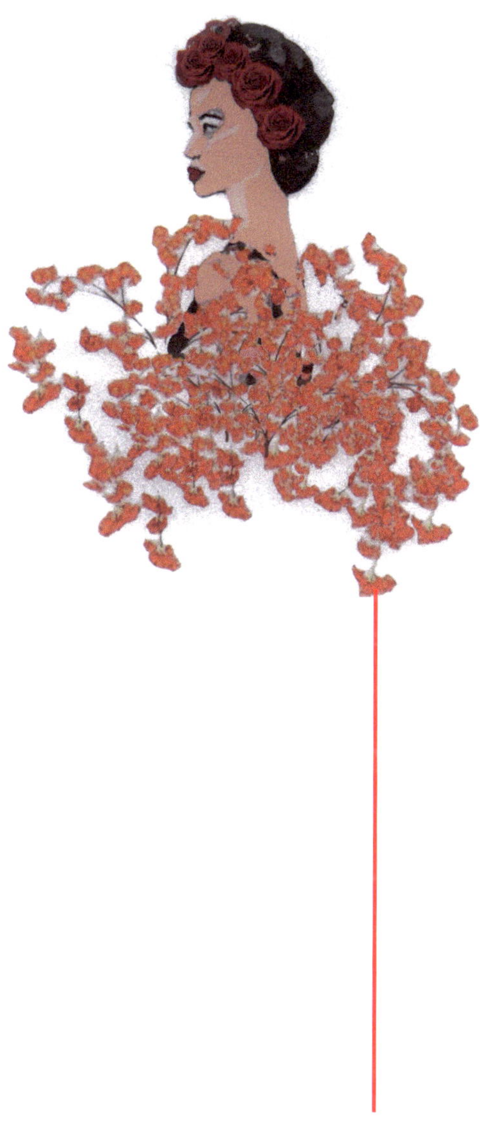

We shall be together darling
To talk to each other
To know ourselves completely
To break any doubts (if any)
To understand
What the future means for us
And to laugh together
With happiness

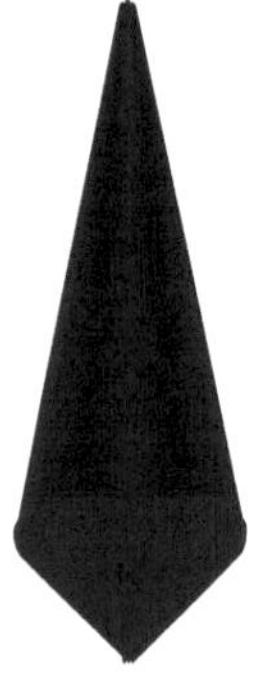

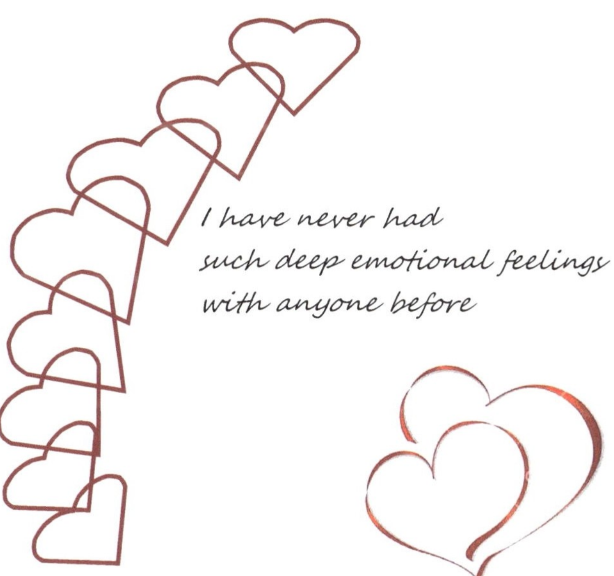

I have never had
such deep emotional feelings
with anyone before

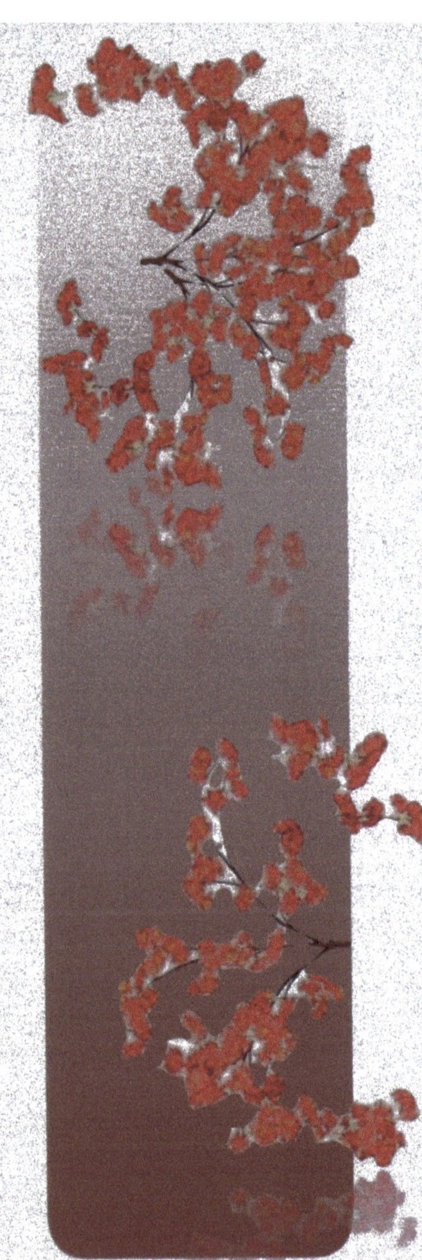

Words

Words can keep forever
bring you close together
Words can mend and bend
hold you 'til the end
Words can disillusion
cause untold confusion
Make you happy make you sad
see the good and see the bad
Piece together what's undone
tell you you're the only one
But none can touch
the word of truth
that stands so tall above
Close your eyes move your lips
and say LOVE LOVE LOVE

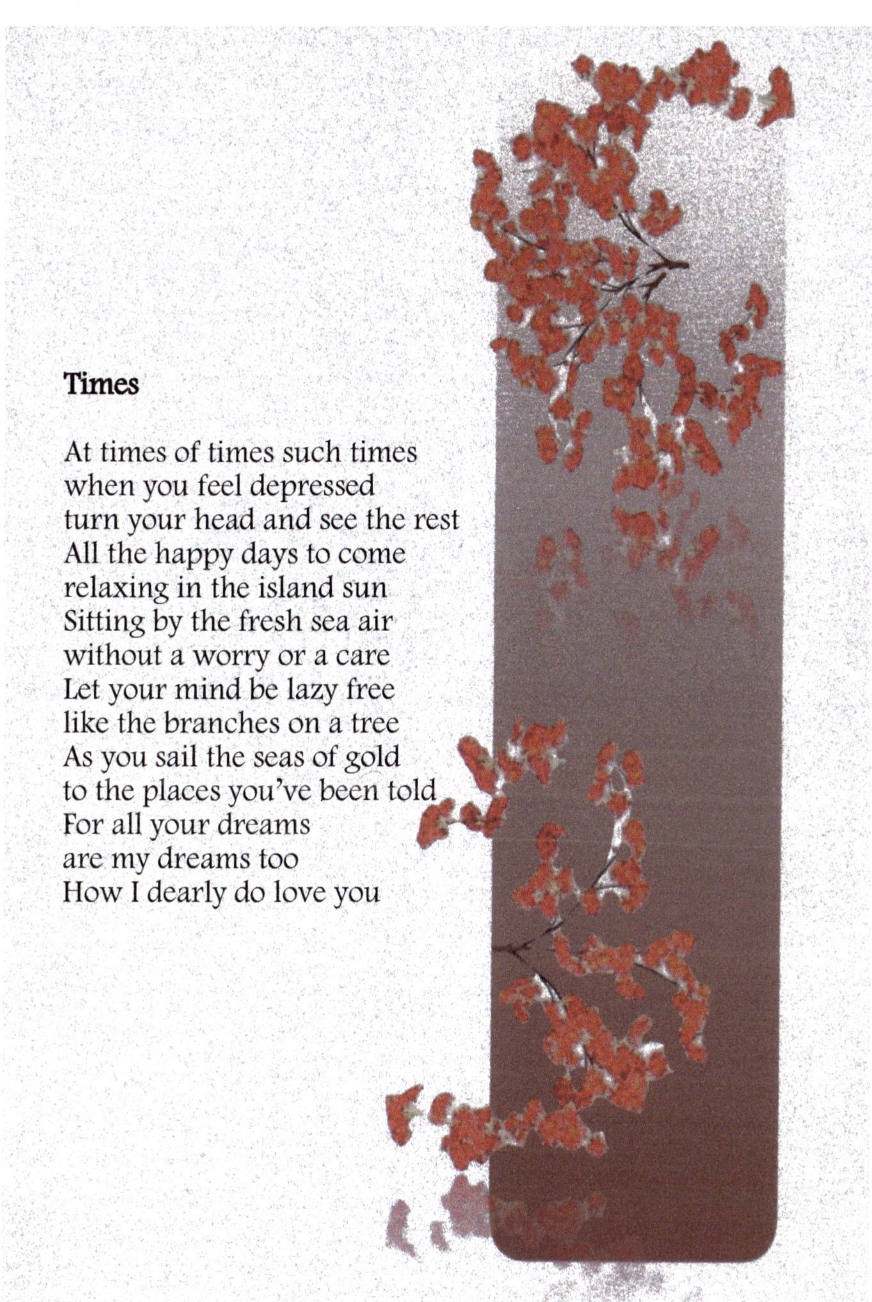

Times

At times of times such times
when you feel depressed
turn your head and see the rest
All the happy days to come
relaxing in the island sun
Sitting by the fresh sea air
without a worry or a care
Let your mind be lazy free
like the branches on a tree
As you sail the seas of gold
to the places you've been told
For all your dreams
are my dreams too
How I dearly do love you

I Adore You

I adore you
I adore your eyes
Your nose your mouth
Your cheeky smile
Your giggly laugh
I adore you
Because you're you

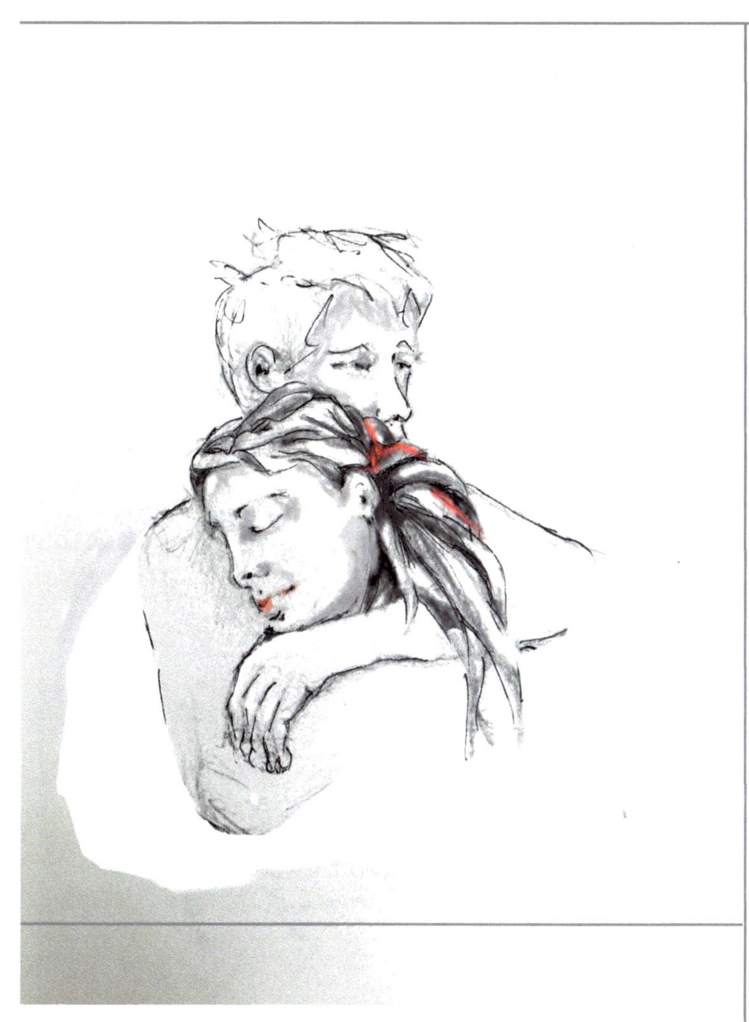

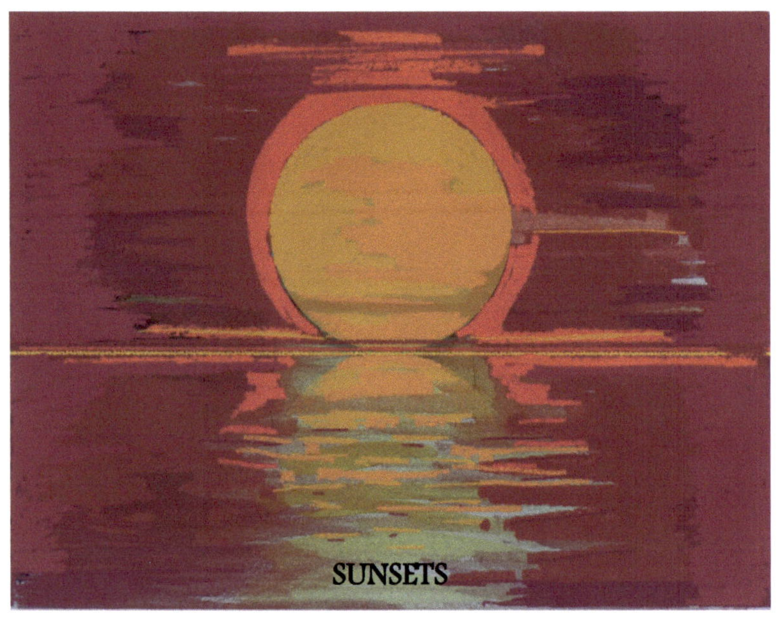

Golden sunsets rest across your shoulder
over radiant glowing seas
Apple blossoms fall when they're older
from emerald sunlit trees

When we're together
there is that special feeling
binding us
we both know it

It's been so many
    We've both missed

..........but we have the rest

*weeks darling
each other.........*

of our lives to   love ♥

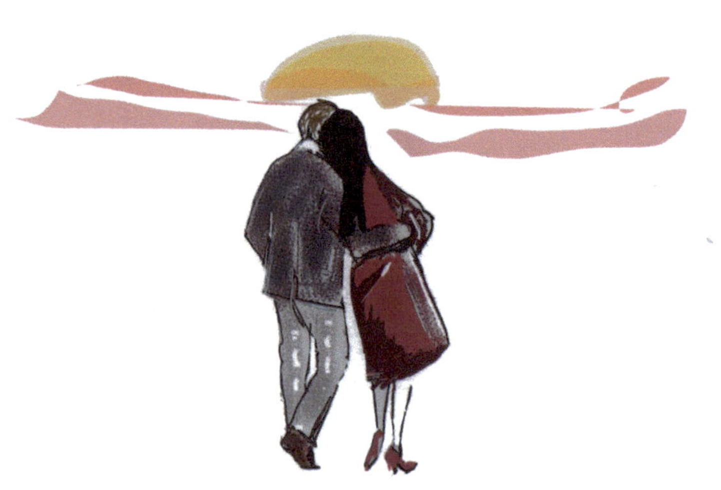

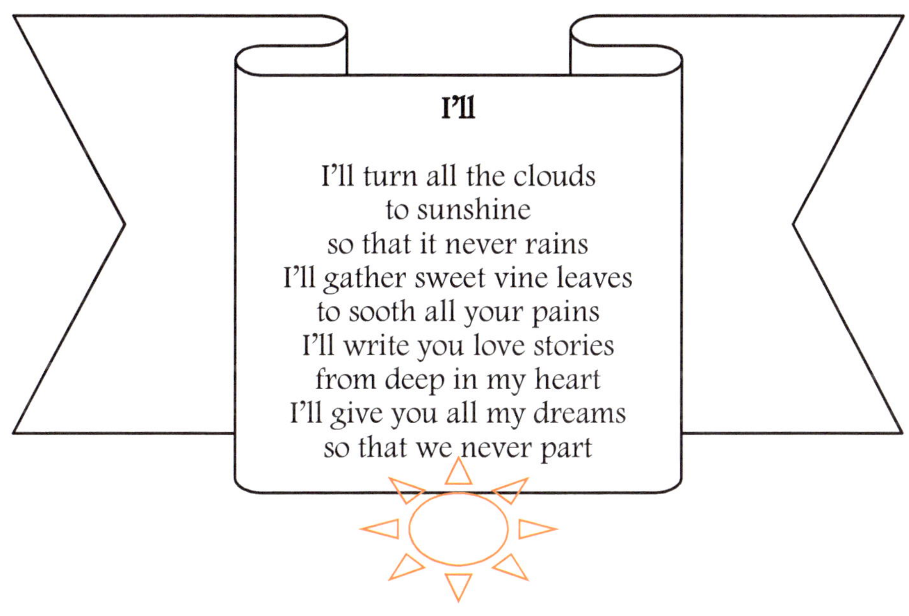

I'll

I'll turn all the clouds
to sunshine
so that it never rains
I'll gather sweet vine leaves
to sooth all your pains
I'll write you love stories
from deep in my heart
I'll give you all my dreams
so that we never part

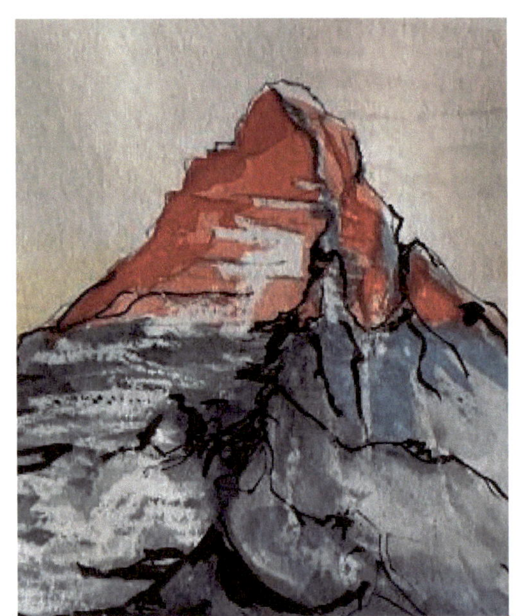

MOUNTAINS

To the tops of mountains
We shall fly
To reach the sun
Beyond the sky
In our search
For all the reasons why

Yes, we shall get there
Past the far horizons
And never once look back
Not even for one
Fraction of a moment

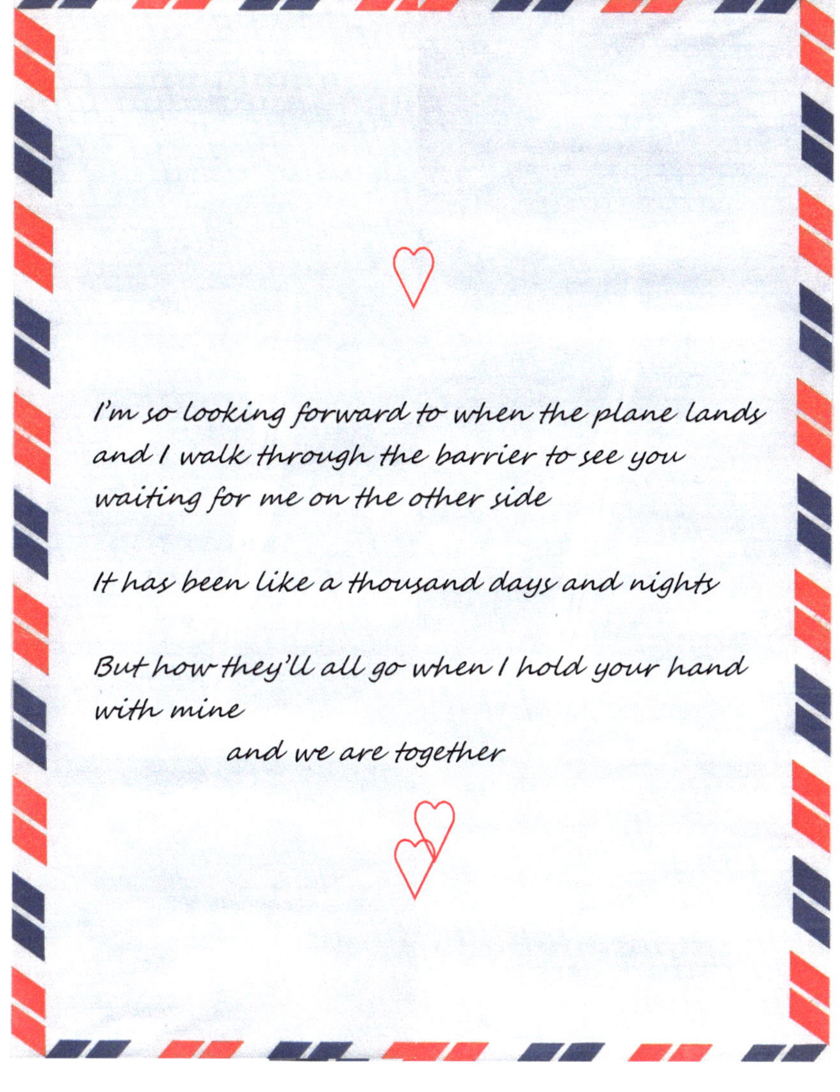

I'm so looking forward to when the plane lands
and I walk through the barrier to see you
waiting for me on the other side

It has been like a thousand days and nights

But how they'll all go when I hold your hand
with mine
          and we are together

Touching

Touching
In a daydream glow
Touching
Letting all your feelings show
Petting not forgetting
Loving is for real
Holding close together
The feelings that you feel
Graciously and modest
In every kind of way
Love is now forever
Not only for today
Touching
Seeking every sunrise
Walking in the sand
In times of trouble
Holding each others hand
Reaching for a mountain
That's way above the sky
Knowing you will make it
You're really going to try
Touching
Being ready to fly

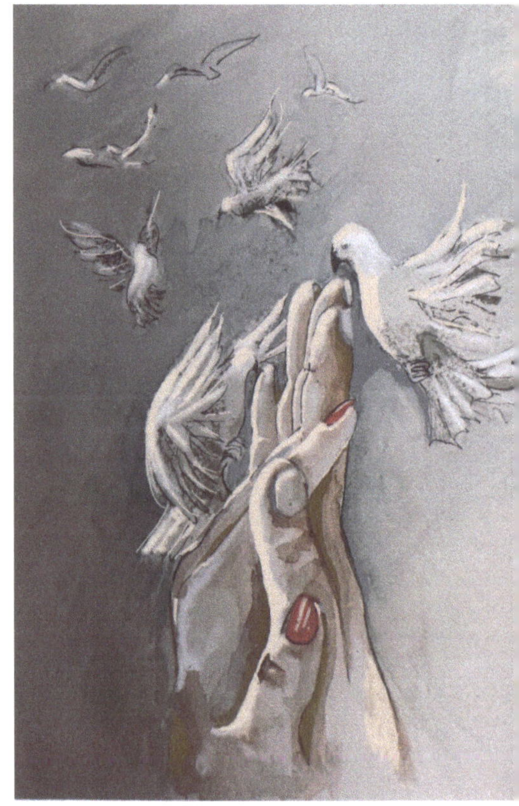

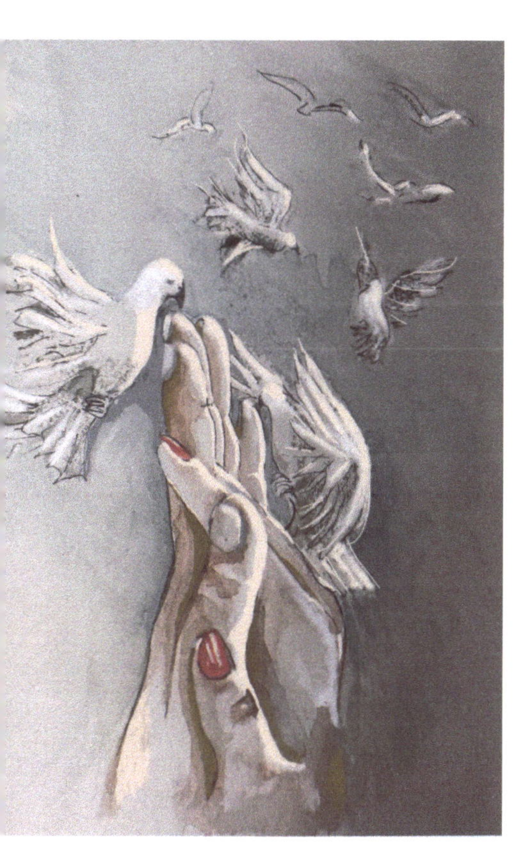

Sublime

You my precious pearl
Light my life with sunshine
Glow with every moonshine
Take shadows from the daytime
And make my world sublime

It's wonderful to have this much love for

to love you this much

its wonderful to have

this much love for

in time you too will realise

to love you this much

this much love for someone

to love you

it's also wonderful for someone

it's also won

wonderful to have

you too will realise

This much

much love for someone

you too will realise

you too will

This much

much love for someone

to love you this much

its wonderful to have

this much love for

to love you this much

this much love for someone

to love you

this much love for someone

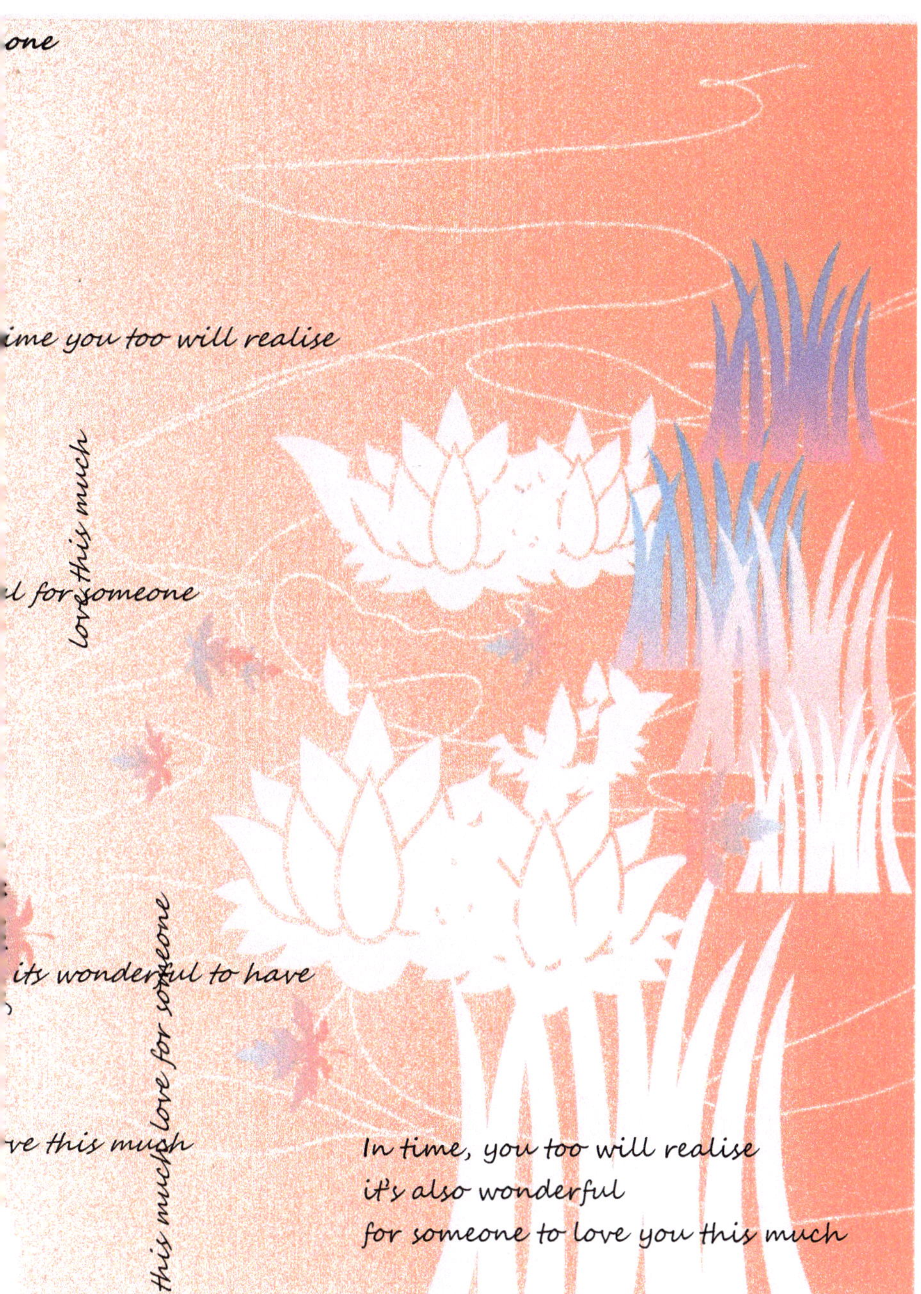
one
ime you too will realise
love this much
l for someone
its wonderful to have
love for someone
ve this much
this much love for someone
In time, you too will realise
it's also wonderful
for someone to love you this much

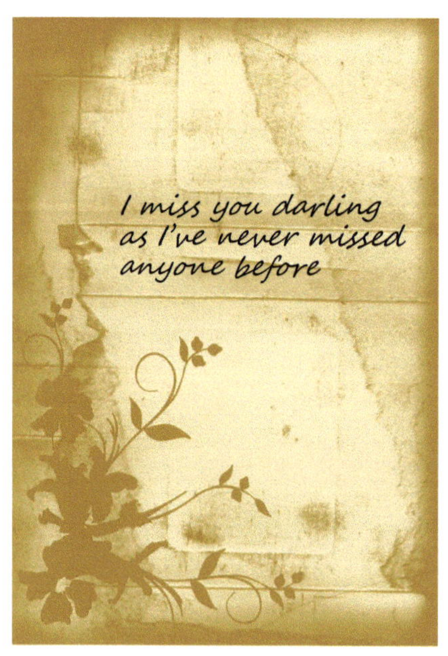

121

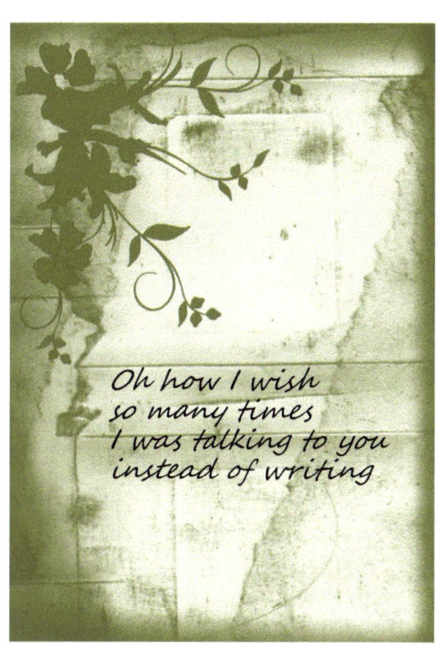

Oh how I wish
so many times
I was talking to you
instead of writing

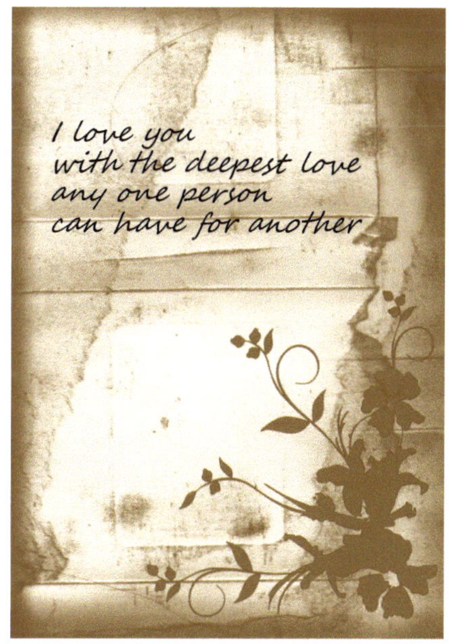

I love you
with the deepest love
any one person
can have for another

Let's Turn a Page

Let's turn a page
to read a book
and find the words
you've never heard
then turn just once again
as though to turn a life
within the written word
or part of what it seems
to reveal another segment
of our forever dreams
to place yourself upon the page
as though you're there alone
and vanish between the lines
like water on a stone
then you become the story
the other persons dreams
all part of what it seems
and if the story be of love
once you have gone within
it's really up to you to feel
to make the story in the book
something that you only read
or something that is real

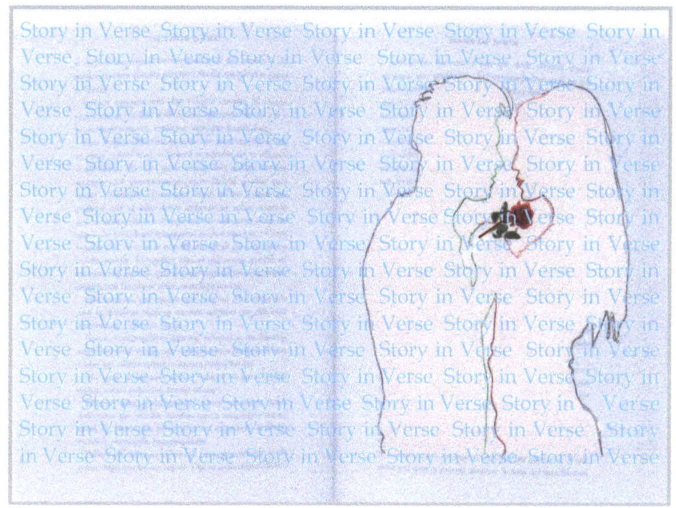

LIKE PIECES OF A PUZZLE
WORDS LINK US TOGETHER

Know me now as you always shall
For my love will always be real
And as strong for you.................for being you

Darling, life is so short
        But how wonderful if you can share it
                with someone
                    you
                absolutely love

I KNOW NOW

I know now
As I've never known before
What to live a life really means
What makes you want
to share your land
When you find that special something
And hold it tight within your hand
To realise all the reasons
Not just for what is now
But a being and a knowing
That will not change within the seasons

I know now
As I've never known before
What it is to want to give
That helps you how to understand
When you find that special something
And hold it tight within your hand
Revealing all the scenes
That make it reality
To be a part of life
Beyond the distance of your dreams

All The Time

All the time
We were together
We didn't mention love
We didn't have to
It was always there
Throughout the years
Running through our veins

Love is..........

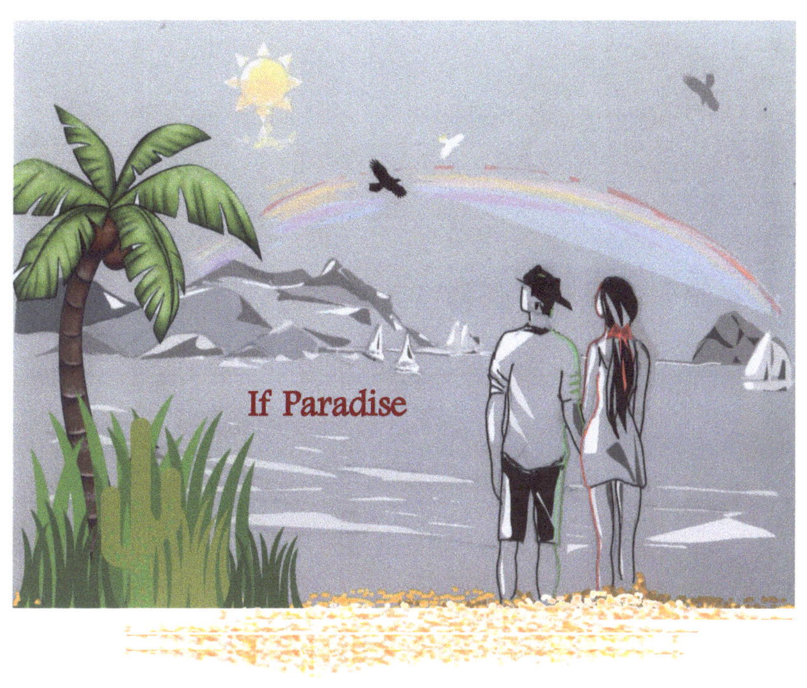

If Paradise is all it means
Then you are captured in my dreams
As rainbows sweep across the sky
I discover all the reasons why
Deep inside the colour zone
Wonderlands begin to clone
All the lilies on the lake
Gather round to contemplate
As wishes float upon the shore
Our hands outstretch for more
Gold dust falls around our feet
The taste of everything so sweet
Locked within the scenes
The paradise of all our dreams

Do You Remember

Here we sit
watching our children
and their children's children

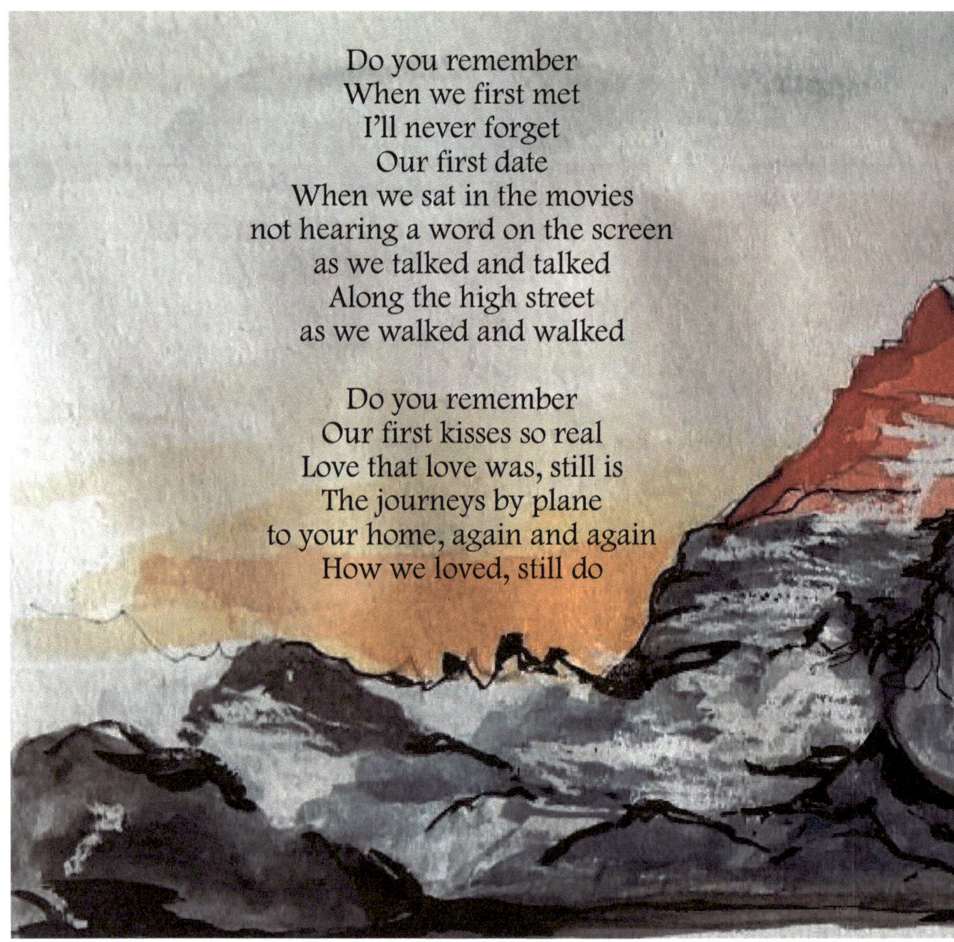

That I be loved by you
Is all I ever ask for

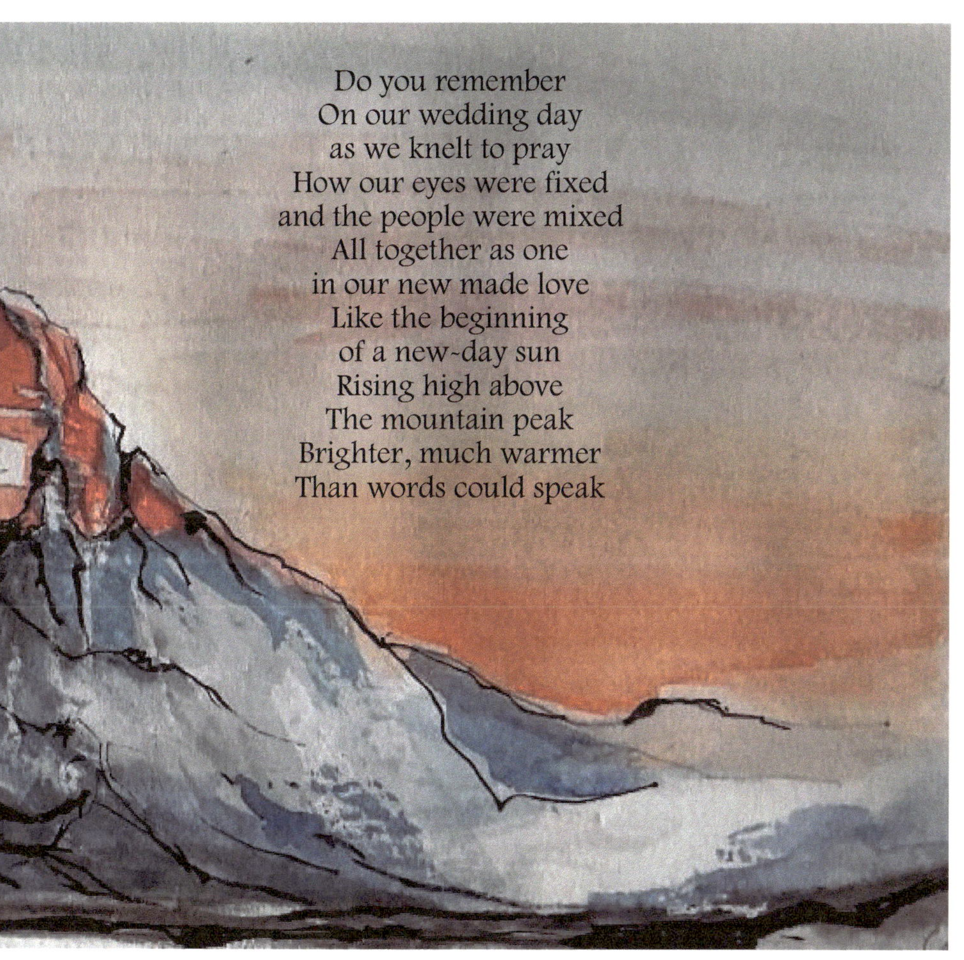

Do you remember
On our wedding day
as we knelt to pray
How our eyes were fixed
and the people were mixed
All together as one
in our new made love
Like the beginning
of a new~day sun
Rising high above
The mountain peak
Brighter, much warmer
Than words could speak

You will always be loved by me

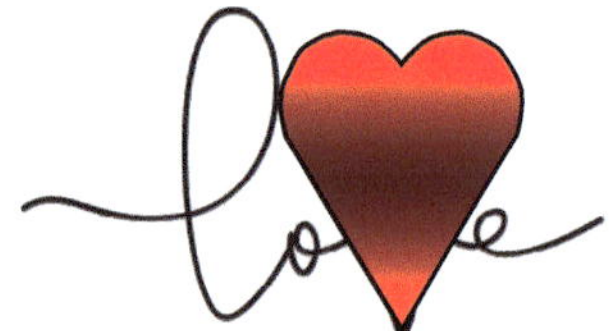

LOVE

LOVE SPREADS ITS WINGS

FAR BEYOND AND WIDE

WORDS ARE LOVINGLY WRITTEN

WITH PASSION AND WITH PRIDE

KNOWING THAT YOU'LL BE THERE

FOREVER BY MY SIDE

EASY DAYS ROLL ON BY

OTHERS HINGE BATTERED LIKE A ROCK

WHEN TWO AND TWO MAKE ONE

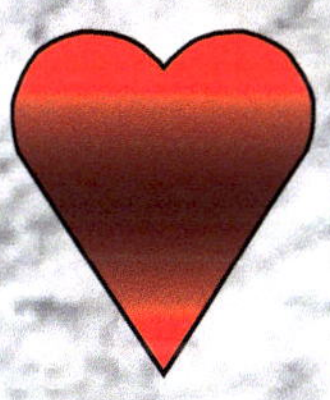

TIME TICK-TOCK DOESN'T STOP

THE LINES OF LIFE DESCEND

HEARTS CAN ALWAYS BREAK AND MEND

TRUTH STANDS STILL AROUND THE CORNER

THE WORDS IN MY BOOK RELIVE IT TO THE END

with LOVE with LOVE with LOVE with LOVE with LOVE with LOVE with LOVE wit
with LOVE with LOVE with LOVE with LOVE with LOVE with LOVE with LOVE wit
with LOVE with LOVE with LOVE with LOVE with LOVE with LOVE with LOVE wit
with LOVE with LOVE with LOVE with LOVE with LOVE with LOVE with LOVE wit
with LOVE with LOVE with LOVE with LOVE with LOVE with LOVE with LOVE wit
LOVE with LOVE with LOVE with LOVE with LOVE with LOVE with LOVE with LO
with LOVE with LOVE with LOVE with LOVE with LOVE with LOVE with LOVE wit
LOVE with LOVE with LOVE with LOVE with LOVE with LOVE with LOVE with LO
with LOVE with LOVE with LOVE with LOVE with LOVE with LOVE with LOVE wit
LOVE with LOVE with LOVE with LOVE with LOVE with LOVE with LOVE with LO
with LOVE with LOVE with LOVE with LOVE with LOVE with LOVE with LOVE wit
LOVE with LOVE with LOVE with LOVE with LOVE with LOVE with LOVE with LO
with LOVE with LOVE with LOVE with LOVE with LOVE with LOVE with LOVE wit
LOVE with LOVE with LOVE with LOVE with LOVE with LOVE with LOVE with I
LOVE with LOVE with LOVE with LOVE with LOVE with LOVE with LOVE with LO

with LOVE with LOVE with LOVE with
LOVE with LOVE with LOVE with LOV
LOVE with LOVE with LOVE with LOVI
with LOVE with LOVE with LOVE with
LOVE with LOVE with LOVE with LOVI
with LOVE with LOVE with LOVE with
LOVE with LOVE with LOVE with LOVI
with LOVE with LOVE with LOVE with

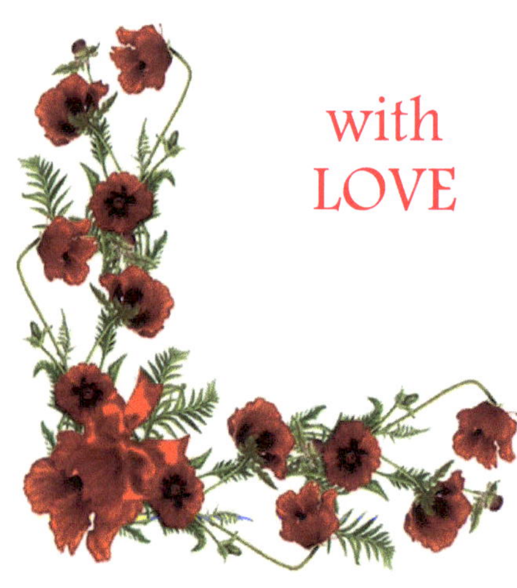

with
LOVE

133

VE with LOVE with LOVE with LOVE with LOVE with LOVE with LOVE
VE with LOVE with LOVE with LOVE with LOVE with LOVE with LOVE
VE with LOVE with LOVE with LOVE with LOVE with LOVE with LOVE
VE with LOVE with LOVE with LOVE with LOVE with LOVE with LOVE
VE with LOVE with LOVE with LOVE with LOVE with LOVE with LOVE with LOVE with
th LOVE with LOVE with LOVE with LOVE with LOVE with LOVE with LOVE with LOVE
VE with LOVE with LOVE with LOVE with LOVE with LOVE with LOVE with LOVE with
th LOVE **with LOVE** with LOVE with LOVE with LOVE with LOVE with LOVE with LOVE
VE with LOVE with LOVE with LOVE with LOVE with LOVE with LOVE with LOVE with
th LOVE with LOVE with LOVE with LOVE with LOVE with LOVE with LOVE with LOVE
VE with LOVE with LOVE with LOVE with LOVE with LOVE with LOVE with LOVE with
th LOVE with LOVE with LOVE with LOVE with LOVE with LOVE with LOVE with LOVE
VE with LOVE with LOVE with LOVE with LOVE with LOVE with LOVE with LOVE with
   with LOVE with LOVE with LOVE with LOVE with LOVE with LOVE with LOVE with
th LOVE with LOVE with LOVE with LOVE with LOVE with LOVE with LOVE with LOVE
E with LOVE with LOVE with LOVE with LOVE with LOVE with LOVE with LOVE with
h LOVE with LOVE with with LOVE with LOVE with LOVE with LOVE with LOVE with
h LOVE with LOVE with LOVE with LOVE with LOVE with LOVE **with LOVE** with LOVE
E with LOVE with LOVE with LOVE with LOVE with LOVE with LOVE with LOVE with
h LOVE with LOVE with LOVE with LOVE with LOVE with LOVE with LOVE with LOVE
E with LOVE with LOVE with LOVE with LOVE with LOVE with LOVE with LOVE with
h LOVE with LOVE with LOVE with LOVE with LOVE with LOVE with LOVE with LOVE
E with LOVE with LOVE with LOVE with LOVE with LOVE with LOVE with LOVE with

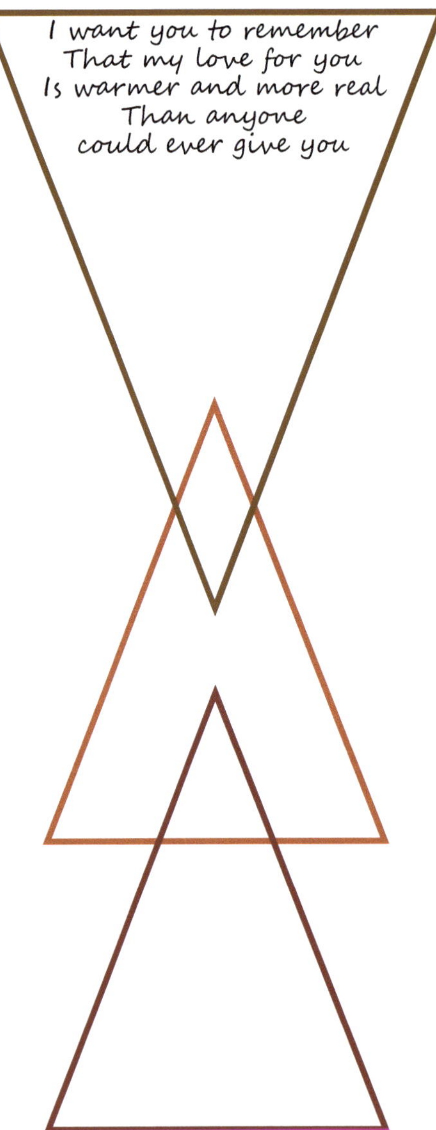

I want you to remember
That my love for you
Is warmer and more real
Than anyone
could ever give you

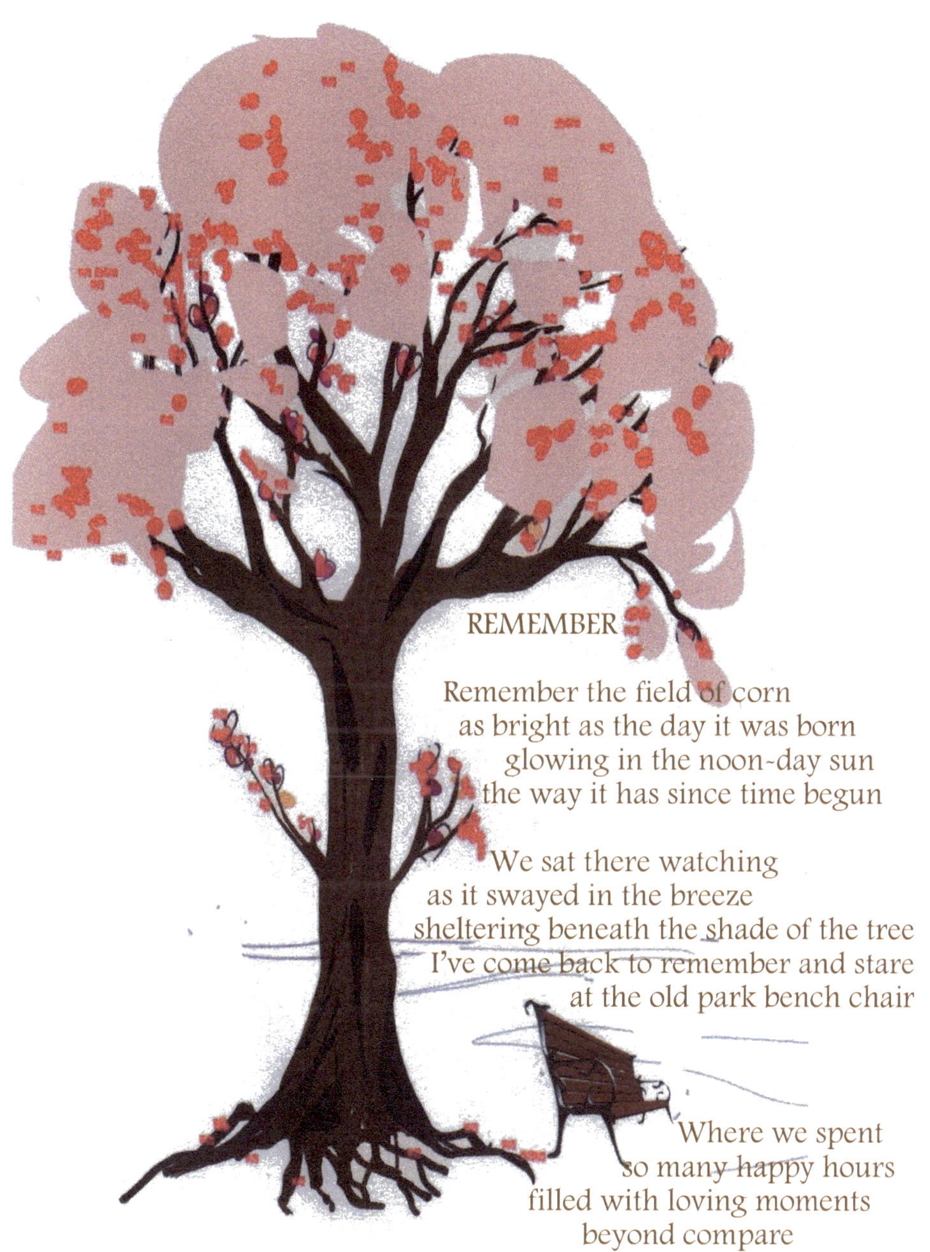

REMEMBER

Remember the field of corn
as bright as the day it was born
glowing in the noon-day sun
the way it has since time begun

We sat there watching
as it swayed in the breeze
sheltering beneath the shade of the tree
I've come back to remember and stare
at the old park bench chair

Where we spent
so many happy hours
filled with loving moments
beyond compare

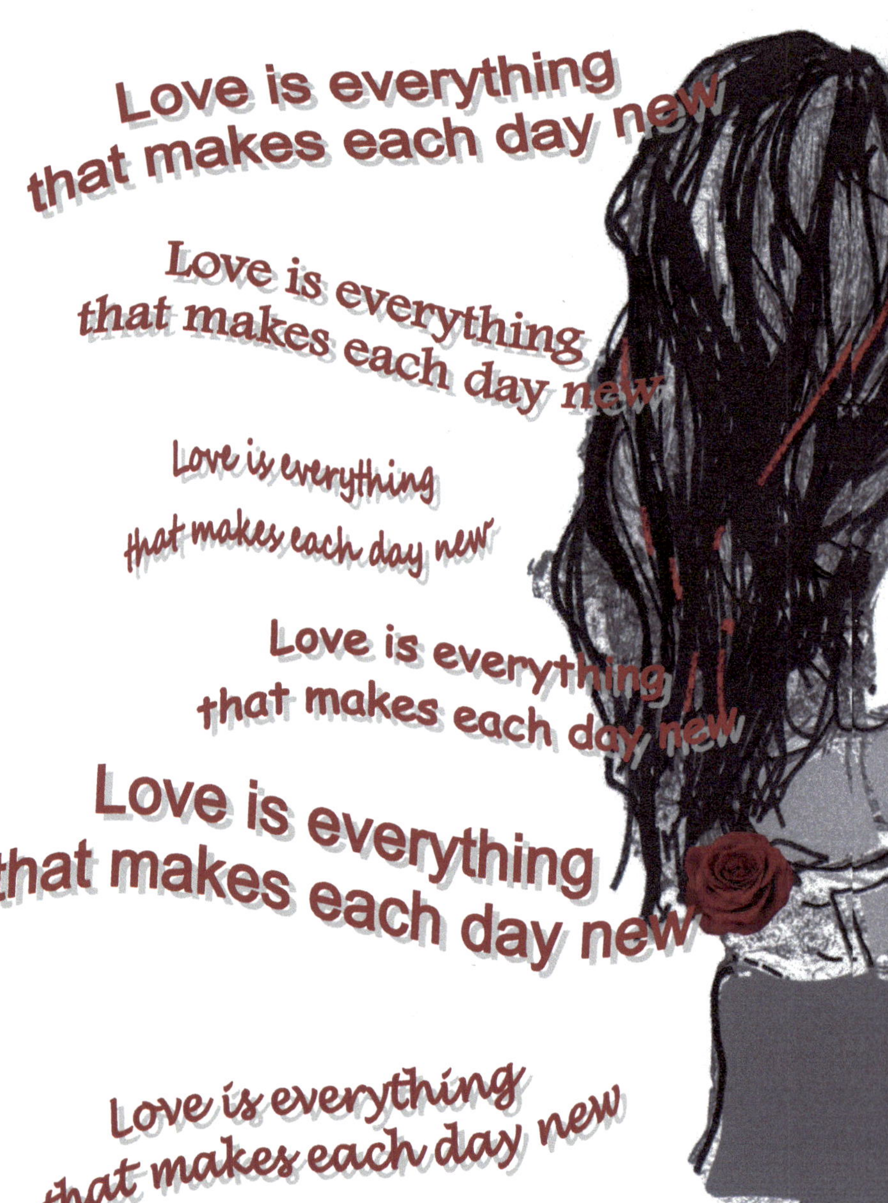

Love is everything
that makes each day new

Love is everything
that makes each day new

Love is everything
that makes each day new

Love is everything
that makes each day new

Love is everything
that makes each day new

Love is everything
that makes each day new

Love is everything
that makes each day new

Love is everything
that makes each day new

Love is everything
that makes each day new

Love is everything
that makes each day new

Love is everything
that makes each day new

Believe in all
Don't change
Because that's what

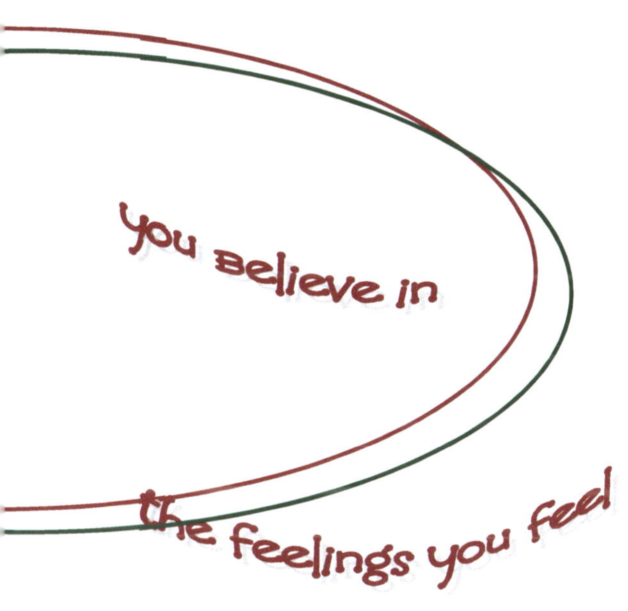

you believe in
the feelings you feel
you know is real

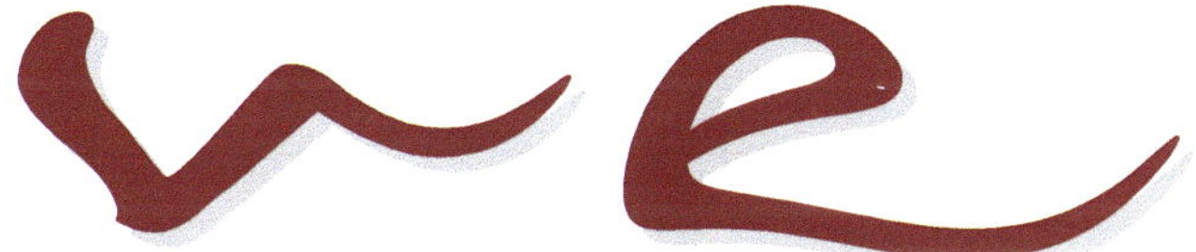

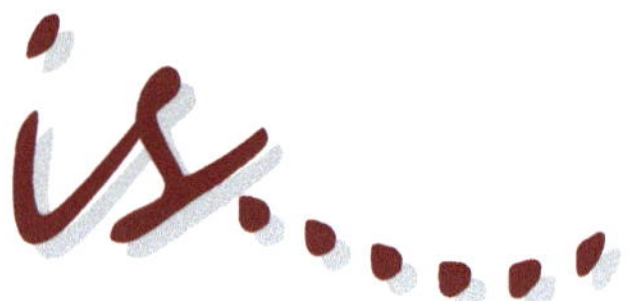

Story in Verse Story in Verse Story in Verse
Story in Verse Story in Verse Story in Verse
Story in Verse Story in Verse Story in Verse
Story in Verse Story in Verse Story in Verse
Story in Verse Story in Verse Story in Verse
Story in Verse Story in Verse Story in Verse
Story in Verse Story in Verse Story in Verse
Story in Verse Story in Verse Story in Verse
Story in Verse Story in Verse Story in Verse
Story in Verse Story in Verse Story in Verse
Story in Verse Story in Verse Story in Verse in
Verse Story in Verse Story in Verse Story in
Verse Story in Verse Story in Verse Story in
Verse Story in Verse Story in Verse Story in
Verse Story in Verse Story in Verse Story in
Verse Story in Verse Story in Verse Story in
Verse Story in Verse Story in Verse Story in
Verse Story in Verse Story in Verse Story in
Verse Story in Verse Story in Verse Story in

Just the 2 of us
Is all it takes
Just the 2 of US
Is what it makes

Roy Benson's career has taken him though the entire scope of the entertainment business as Producer, Director, Writer and Editor.

He worked on editing some of the most successful films ever made, including 7 Oscar winner *Lawrence of Arabia* directed by **David Lean**, *Dr Strangelove* directed by **Stanley Kubrick**, and *Yentl* directed by **Barbra Streisand**. Other major Feature Films he has worked on the editing are: *The Bedford Incident,* (Directed 2nd Unit battle scenes), *The War Lover, Death Wish, A Hard Day's Night, and An American Werewolf in London.*

The Beatles asked him to edit their film *Magical Mystery Tour,* which led to him directing and editing a number of musical promo films, working with **Paul McCartney** for some time.

He has written book and libretto for his stage musicals *EARTH* - A Universal Musical Experience, and *Broken Blossoms* - A love story set in the era of the Samurai wars, which he hopes to produce in the near future

As Producer he is setting up his own movie projects. *John Harold's Circus* an animated musical fantasy with several songs. He has written the script/ libretto for *The Prince of Pluto and The Wicked Galaxy Queen and The Milky Way War* animated rock musical feature.

Roy was Production Supervisor on *To End All Wars, Until Death* with **Jean-Claude Van Damme**, worked in Bangkok on *Rambo* with **Sylvester Stallone**, *Killing Season* with **Robert De Niro** and **John Travolta**.

With his graphic design expertise he has created a series of 10 themed poetry books 'Story in Verse': *Love is..., Just the 2 of US, 'til the end of time, Memories are Forever, Beyond the Clouds, Love Transcends,   all of me loves all of you, Silent Snowdrops, Past Lives, LYRICS of LOVE.*

His latest venture *METROPOLIS* is a stage musical based on the famous silent movie, to be performed in black & white.

About the Illustrator

Christine Banat is a Surrey based artist specialising in figurative art.
Having run a successful Interior Design business for many years, painting had always been a background love as she was creating and selling work.

In 2020 Christine began to focus on developing her painting skills, resulting in her being accepted onto a Masters Degree in a Fine Art course at the UCA Farnham.

During this time her work was shown to Roy Benson, who was looking for illustrators who could create drawings and paintings for his thousands of poems to be published in a series of 10 themed books 'Story in Verse'. The first being 'Love is'.

Once Christine was introduced to the project she began to understand what was required, and started working with Roy developing a style of illustration which could express the story of the love and closeness he enjoyed during his long marriage to Nancy, that is conveyed so beautifully in his poems.